Nicholas deVore III
Photographer

Box 812 / Aspen, Colorado U.S.A. 81611 / Telephone 303 / 925-2317

Subsistence U.S.A.

Text by Carol Hill
Photographs by Bruce Davidson

A Subsistence Press Book

Holt, Rinehart and Winston
New York, Chicago, San Francisco

Copyright 1973 in all countries of the International Copyright Union by Subsistence Press, Inc. and Holt, Rinehart and Winston, Inc. All rights reserved, including the right of reproduction in whole or in part. Prepared and produced by Subsistence Press, Inc. Published in the United States of America in 1973 by Holt, Rinehart and Winston, Inc., Publishers, 383 Madison Avenue, New York, New York 10017, U.S.A. Published simultaneously in Canada by Holt, Rinehart and Winston of Canada, Limited.
Library of Congress Catalog Card Number: 73-759
ISBN: 0-03-091223-7 (clothbound)   ISBN: 0-03-091222-9 (paperbound)
Produced by Arthur Gubernick
Printed in Holland by Joh. Enschedé & Zonen, Haarlem
Designed by Samuel N. Antupit

Subsistence U.S.A.

Foreword

In the spring of 1971 Bruce Davidson and I were asked to explore with a camera and a tape recorder, some aspects of American life characterized by the concept of subsistence. In the course of the year and a half of work on the book, we experienced this word in constant, and sometimes tortuous, evolution. Each time we discovered someone who, we thought, should be a part of this book, we found we had to expand or revise our definition of what its subject was. Subsistence came to include principles of survival, originality, wholeness, and independence.

We also discovered that often, the more difficulty we had deciding what people were, the more they belonged in this volume. It is a cliché to state that people cannot be classified, but I don't think any of us ever appreciated the force of that cliché until it was demonstrated again and again by the strength, imagination, humor, and sometimes just plain orneriness of the people in this book.

We traveled all over the country in search of our subjects. We talked to farmers and trappers, schoolteachers and hobos, prisoners and hitchhikers, islanders, street people, black people, white people, and Indians. We traveled to Maine, Georgia, Tennessee, Colorado, Texas, and California.

We wanted the words of the book to be mostly the words of the people we talked to, and the tape recorder was invaluable for this. But it was also burdensome, because you can't select from a conversation as you are having it; and consequently there were reams of transcripts that had to be carefully edited so as to reduce the volume, yet not lose the spirit of the voice. That work was done by Jamie Shalleck.

We spent many hours in travel and talk, trying to define our subject; but it was finally the people in this book who showed us what it was. Subsistence is a synonym for existence, differing only in its suggestion of endurance. So endurance became the subject of this book, the endurance of those who seem to find an extraordinary strength in their experience of themselves. They contradict romantic notions and confirm a tautology as truth: it is endurance that makes them endure. Courage is part of this, but not the usual heroic conception of it. It is rather courage of the small, daily, domestic variety that gives force to lives. The people here reveal that finally the race is not always to the swift; it is the dogged who survive the rugged route.

For one or two people in this book, the decision to live life on their own terms appears self-conscious. In most cases, there is not a decision in the usual sense at all, but only a life lived in accordance with what these people are—people whose endurance, courage, and survival is finally as natural and redeeming as the rising of the sun.

—Carol Hill

7.

Baxter, Maine

The road to Baxter out of Portland cuts through Falmouth on the bay, through the rugged rocks of Maine's famed coast, passing white sails on the water, passing dunes and trees and fisherman's wharves, lobster pots and cribs, clam diggers with pails, and boatmen with sneakers and sunbleached wives, passing nets and pulleys and signs for bait. And then a spin around a cloverleaf, a quick turn down an asphalt stretch to dirt and powdered driving. No sidewalks, signs, or even gravel, just the slow turning of dust, passing small, old farmhouses, set in half used pasture land and trees. The remnants of once rich farming now turned over to people with countryhouse longings and poor folks getting by in an old house on an unpaved road.

You hear a lot in Maine about her people, their stubbornness and pride, their independence, which verges on orneriness. But you hear something new in the voices now—concern for a fading profile. You hear sadness for a life style gone by, with the small farmer dying out, with the pollution in the water making the lobsters die. Industrial pollution is killing the lobsters, and industrial finance is killing farmers, mostly by destroying their independence. "You get big or you get out," some of them will tell you now, still puzzling how it all happened as they turn to look over the land they lost. It's deceitful, farming, for a man can make a go of it in potatoes for twenty years, and then all of a sudden these last five, it's different. It gets harder and harder until one day he's lost his farm and all his equipment, and only his friends save the mortgage on his house. It's deceitful, farming, for how can a man imagine poverty when he's jugging in the buckseat of a tractor, riding through acres of waving, green plants, the ground damp and fragrant from the dew the night before. For a man can be poor, but as long as he's planting his own food, he doesn't feel he owes.

And it is that, as much as anything, that still seems to guarantee a special freedom in working your own land. And it is that, as much as anything, that sent Eric Willoby and his wife back to the land, not so much to farm, but just to take three acres out there in Baxter and raise enough for themselves, making a last attempt to seize on the fast disappearing, self-sufficient life. They knew it would be hard, but they wanted to do that, because that was what they knew how to do—knew how to take old things, old ways of living, and make them work, knew how to plant seeds in the ground and make them grow, knew how to do things like they did it forty years ago—and they decided to live that way.

Their house is old and simple; and when they moved in, they had to stay with neighbors because there was no caulking on the windows, half the glass was out, and it didn't have the doors on. It gets to forty below in those parts in the winter, and Mr. Willoby said the wind blew from one side right out the other. At first the house wasn't anything more than a place for the outside to rest in. But the Willobys had built their first house by going out to the woods with a cross saw and getting it; so they figured they could patch one up as easy as they could start again.

The Willobys are as close to pioneers as this century will permit. They need little from the store. Their one need is gasoline; and if there were a way to do what they have to do with a horse, they'd do it. But Mr. Willoby's greatest achievement, which he recites with knee-slapping glee, is that he beat out the Central Maine Power Company. Because of the way that dependencies determine a world, Mr. Willoby was out to lick Maine Power. And he did. "Harness the wind," he said, and he wrote to the government for a pamphlet on how to build a windmill, studied it, and then sent his son out to the woods for the right kind of lumber and told him to follow instructions on how to carve the blades. Mr. Willoby built the windmill by the pamphlet, and then being a natural mechanic and a man who comes from a long line of blacksmiths, he found it no trouble at all to attach a generator and hook up storage batteries. Now Mr. Willoby slaps his thigh and fills the kitchen with his "Hah!" when the wind clicks through his windmill and all the lights go on.

"Folks lose touch with things," Mrs. Willoby says, "don't know how to do things for themselves anymore." And then she leans back in her rocking chair and looks at the wood stove in the middle of the kitchen and tells the story of how her son-in-law looked at the stove, puzzled, and asked how do you regulate the heat? And maybe there was something of the mother-in-law in her response, but mostly it was her despair for persons in the modern world, when she explained that you didn't regulate it, and it didn't have a regulator, because all you had to do when it got too hot was to open the door until it cooled down.

The Willobys look like a soft and happy vision of America one never saw in the paintings of Grant Wood. Mr. Willoby is wiry, strong, and has straight black hair. His face is ruddy, and the night I arrive, his vitality seems as strong as his humor, which makes the floor shake. Mrs. Willoby has just gotten back from the flea market, held every weekend, where she stands at a table to sell her wares: junk from an old house they had bought and sold ("We didn't make much on it; it was just a bad deal all the way around") and knitting ("I set and knit and knit and knit. I get up at five-thirty in the mornin and knit. I keep ahead of em down there"). She is tired tonight, and her tall, slender form seems to fold right into the arc of the rocking chair. Her fine, blonde hair slips from its bun, and she retrieves it, pushing it back as she wonders why anyone would want to interview them.

It is a moonlit August evening, and Mr. Willoby offers to take me to the spring for some water. We walk down through the meadow past the crickets, the dog leaping and barking, until we get to the spring, where the dog drinks first, then me. Mr. Willoby drinks with pleasure, then fills his jug and tells me he'd sell some of his water in New York if he knew how. When we get back to the house, Mrs. Willoby pulls her chair close to the stove. Although very generous about my coming at the end of a long day, she is a little nervous and fingers the buttons on her sweater while Mr. Willoby snaps his cap across his knee. Then Mrs. Willoby leans back and starts rocking in the chair, while the dog tends to her puppies and the sun throws long shadows on the house.

Eric and Sara Willoby

ERIC: Let me tell you somethin I think probably you're tryin to dig out of us. I can tell ya in five minutes, I think. Um. You see, she and I are the kind of people that have tried fer, well, we'll say fifteen, twenty, thirty years, to do somethin with a business, this kind of construction business, see, like I tried to do. Well, I did all right for a while when my brother was in business drillin wells and we were, ah, and we dig a lot of ditchin and so on so forth. But I find now I'm old enough to realize all of this: if you do not find the thing that you're supposed to do in life or you take one track, which was in the excavatin business, and you go up that track, and if you don't find somebody that you can git good jobs from—and one good job will lead to another so that you can progress yourself up the line—or whether you have to be crooked in order to do this or what it takes to git up to the top, as far as some sort of business like that . . .

11.

We got sick and that ruined me for ten years. So that don't help either. That might have complicated some of it, too. But for some unknown reason, I have an awful lot of good friends. And I was always like my father—I never was too much of a guy to go against anybody. I always wanted to live and let live, you know. And he was that same way, too. And he had a lot of friends, too. So I'd rather keep my friends than to be beatin somebody out of a job or goin up the road givin somebody a hard time. You know what I'm talkin about? And I'd rather be that way and have lots of friends than I would to be a bastard or whatever you call it.

SARA: He got an inner ear infection and dizzy, and he really couldn't do any work at all for almost . . .

ERIC: It took me two years to git out of it, Sara, until I could git back to work.

SARA: I worked as much as I could. Then we lost his father at that time, so that it was quite a turnin point. And we started lookin for places away from where we're livin in Scarborough, because the taxes were gettin so high and everything was gettin beyond.

ERIC: We started in lookin. We were accustomed to payin fifteen dollars on that hundred-acre farm in Scarborough, and then we could see things work up on you until they're eight hundred dollars. Ten years ago we could see this thing comin, so we figured we better get the devil out of Scarborough before they bankrupt us so that we couldn't git out, we wouldn't have the money to move. So we got out of there.

SARA: We have only three acres here. Another hundred acres about four miles from here, you can get hardwood off of. Pulp is growin very strongly on it.

ERIC: With the education and the earnin power that us people have at the age we are, we have a hard job to earn big money. So we figure, well, shoot, we know how to live this way, like we did forty years ago. What's the matter with the way we lived forty years ago? We got through all right. And we can make do ourselves better by havin conveniences like the lectricity out of the wind, you know, a windmill, I mean. We know how to do that now. So we ain't sufferin.

SARA: Like I grow vegetables all summer and can them, and we have them all winter. We have beans, peas, corn, tomatoes, cucumbers, squash, potatoes, kidney beans, baked beans. You name it, we have it. And fruits. We don't have any fruit trees here, but if I can obtain them, I'll can any kind of fruits or anything I can get ahold of. And of course I make jam if I can get hold of the stuff to make it with.

            I don't know as I like doing it, but I know I want to eat next winter. It'll all work, of course, modern way and ours. This is harder.

And everybody says, "Well, I've got a freezer."

Well, fine. I'll get a freezer one day, too. But I can't have a freezer here as yet. So I have to go back to the way I did it thirty years ago.

The doctors told us that this canned goods like this has all the vitamins in it, whereas the frozen ones, you lose all the vitamins. So it's really better for you.

You have your dried beans and everything. Of course you bake beans about every Saturday night. And biscuits. Just about everything that anybody would need to just survive on. We don't raise meat or anything, but we have learned to get by on very little meat. We will buy eggs from our neighbor for fifty cents a dozen, and they're great big eggs, nice fresh ones, you know.

ERIC: We don't mind living this way. We'd just as soon live this way.

SARA: It's a lot of satisfaction.

ERIC: More so than the guy that's got millions. Because the guy that's got millions, he can do anything, can't he. But you got to know how to do something if you're gonna do it this way.

SARA: Like I got a son-in-law, and he don't know how to run this stove.

ERIC: T'ain't complicated.

SARA: I had it going hot one day—it was way over six hundred. He says, "How do you bake? You burn everything up?"

I says, "No, no, you wouldn't."

"Well, how do you do it?"

"Well," I says, "you just open the door a little bit and let some of the heat out."

He still can't figure out how I can bake in that oven. If you want to bake slow, you just don't get it as hot as it is now. You let it simmer down a little bit.

ERIC: You know, you eat out of that stove and there's a hell of a difference between eatin out of that stove and eatin out of an electric one or a gas one. It's the smoke in that thing, you know. It flavors the food. Baking beans in that, there's no comparison. Your bread, your biscuits, and everything all taste better on that old stove.

SARA: Oh yeah. You get her up around six hundred and she'll really cook those biscuits. Oh, and another thing we have—we don't cook em very often but if we're going to have a crowd sometimes we do. And because we have no money to have a big spread, we have a big hole-bean, and we cook them in the ground in the field. You build a hot, hot fire. And get it going good and hot. Soak the beans twenty-four hours. Then put your big iron kettles of beans in the fire and let them stand in it twenty-four hours.

ERIC: You can't cook them in anything else. You've gotta have cast iron.

SARA: And those are the best beans there ever was.

ERIC: The way we live, with the food that we eat, you'll find that the ones like us are better healthy-wise and eatin healthier foods than the rich people are. Because the richer—well, I won't say rich, but I'll say richer people will think of goin to the restaurants and eatin fried foods, like fried steak and French fries, and all those goodies, you know, that we think are goodies, you know, that are expensive of course. And they go, what, two or three times a week to have a steak feed, probably. Now that isn't good for you, too much fried foods. But see, we eat more vegetables and not fried foods, see. We have some, but it isn't nothin probably like what they—I don't know how they live. I know we can't afford . . .

SARA: It makes me feel good to go into the store and see the prices and I don't have to buy it. Of course, you'd like tomatoes and lettuce and cucumbers, fresh, but you just say no. They're too expensive. Just walk by em.

ERIC: There's a lot of people in the State of Maine that live like we do, I believe. As you ride up through the State of Maine, you will see places, and you will want to know how in the devil do they live, you know. You'll go along and you'll see some of those places that really, well, they probably look worse than this one does, and some of them look the way ours is. And you'll wonder how they get along. But you'll find that they'll can things and find it more or less in order to live.

SARA: We're slowly gonna try to fix this house up, and when we get to retirement age, we're hopin to sell and go further into Maine, if we can find a shack somewheres with a few acres of land. Because we don't need this big house, the two of us. This was just sort of an investment, and of course we bought it very reasonable.

When we bought it, this whole foundation was cavin in. And that winter, it it was about thirty to forty below almost all winter. We moved in in December . . .

ERIC: One of the worst winters we ever had.

SARA: And the windows were all out, the door was out, and it was cold. So here we are, tryin to fix this place up, tryin to keep the fire goin, tryin to make it so we can live in it. And we stayed with a neighbor for a little while till we got it so we could live in it, you know. Boy, it was rough. I'm tellin you. I wore insulated underwear, slacks, woolens, because the wind just blew right across.

ERIC: Because the wall was all out, see. These windows were all out. And we came here in December. And the funny thing—when we git talkin about this, Ma always starts in laughin, thinkin about what I said. Well, the windows were all out here, see, where the vandals had taken over, you know. And of course the doors was open and the wind was blowin right straight through, fog and all, you know. And Judas, it was so goddamned cold, you know. "Well naturally," you'd say.

Well, I was in here puttyin, puttyin the glass, you know, where the windows—and tryin to get that stove hooked up, you know. And it was so cold my hands was all numb. I couldn't hardly bend my fingers, see. So naturally I says, "Well for God's sake, Ma, shut the door." And what good did it do to shut the door, wall and windows out? But you know, naturally, you'd just—reflex action, you'd say, "Well, shut the door, Ma, for God's sake!" And here's the wind blowin right through the place anyway. So what difference did it make?

SARA: It was straight, hard work, but it was an enjoyment. I mean, it was a miserable enjoyment, but as you set back now and look at it, you'll laugh because there's a million things that we had to go through.

Like the bathroom. We thought it was workin fine, but then it froze up. So he went and got his steam pump goin and steamed it out.

ERIC: I've got a steam boiler down in the cellar, see, and it heats the house here. We've got steam heat as long as you put the wood to it. So I got that ready. It's on wheels. I put the steam right to the pipe, right out through the pipe. I came up here and I says, "Well, I guess I got that matter all cleaned out and all unthawed." Later I went down and the goddamned water was runnin right into the cellar. Pipe was broke. So that ended that.

SARA: No bathroom, he means. So the next best thing was the two-by-four shack way out in the back of the barn. And that's tiltin like this, so my daughter had named it Tiltin Hilton. So that's what we had to use the rest of the winter. Oh boy, that I didn't like.

ERIC: See, the wall had froze. When the wall pushed in, why it pulled all that pipe apart out there. Well, you couldn't git out there with six feet of frost and dig that pipe up, see, and repair it. So I just plain forgot that bathroom for that winter. The next year we got that and the wall fixed up.

Took me two months. Had to jack the house up. We had to bridge it to hold the house up while we did the foundation.

But the sad part of that was that there's only one of me, and here's the work outside that I could have been doin and makin money, but I got a four-thousand-dollar wall job done underneath my house. But I couldn't eat it that winter. So I lost my work, but I got the wall in. So we suffered that one out for that winter, see. No money for that winter. Usually I do estimatin work, haulin gravel and diggin holes and bulldozin.

SARA: You have to earn enough to get by on, you know.

ERIC: We just ain't got no money. There's just a limited amount to buy what you need. And that's it. And there isn't any money left over to buy all kinds of boats, go down to the ocean and float around in. You don't have those kind of things. There's what you put your money in: them cannin jars over there. You buy the tops and the glass, and well, of course, you have to buy gasoline. And we can't seem to git back further enough to have a horse and raise oats to keep the horse goin, but we have to buy gasoline. But I think it would be too hard to go back too far into this ecology bit.

SARA: There's a point. But you can go so far. You can't go as far in a horse as in a car. Well, you could do it if you wanted to plan your work around it. I think a horse might be cheaper.

ERIC: Well, how would you hook a horse up to a bulldozer or a backhaul?

SARA: You'd have to forget about that. You'd have to go completely into farmin. It's self-survival, I call it. The more you get into this, it's more self-survival. You ain't dependin on the store for too much. Just your flour and your sugar and things like this.

I'm tryin to start a little organic growin, but I'm not progressin too far, because I just started last year. It's gonna take us a few years to get it, and we don't have that much place. Of course, I raked the leaves up and started it, but I haven't progressed too far in it. But I'll work on it. I have my little corner out there, and I'm startin on my own. But I've got to do some more readin in it.

ERIC: It's growin without any fertilizers or anything. And those things, I do believe they really work, that they tell about: if you plant onions alongside of certain vegetables, it keeps the bugs away, like worms out of cabbage and things like that. We've heard this, and Ma's read about it in these books, you know. And I think it really does. And if you prepare your ground, your soil, the way they tell you, that helps keep away the bugs, too. The ground's got to be good and healthy, see. If you take a dog and he's all run down out here, well, the fleas git on him and kill him, right? Or they'll suck the life right out of him, right? Well, the ground is the same way. If you git the ground ready for the plant, to make the plant healthy, why then the plant don't have diseases or bugs or otherwise, see.

17.

SARA: Takes a lot of time to do that. Or else you've got to buy a big shreddin machine. And I ain't gonna buy a two-hundred-dollar shreddin machine. I can wait a
few years. It takes all your waste material and shreds it up. This is part of your organic,
see. And then you put that on your ground and work it in. You know, like say when
you trim a bush out here, you can put your bushes right through it, and it'll shred it up.

ERIC: That hurries it up to get it back into the soil again, natural, see, to
decay it back into the soil. This is the part of the pollution problem that we have, is that
if they could hurry it up with a shredder or somethin and git it back into the soil and
let the soil eat it up and let it oxidize that way, rather than to take it and burn it—well,
that's too fast an oxidation, that burnin business, because it causes the pollution, see. Well,
that isn't the natural way for it to go, see. It's supposed to destroy itself in the ground.
Like when they burn us—I mean, it's the same action: you go back to the soil. So this is
why we're havin this pollution thing, is because everybody's tryin to burn so much dump
all the time.

SARA: Before, when we were tryin to live tip-top, you know, we had a
little extra money comin in—I was workin, he was workin, we had two children and we
lived the modern way, you know. Everything wasn't pushbutton. But we had Central
Maine Electricity and automatic washin machines, TV, and we'd go out more. Now we
very seldom—you can't afford to go out, really. But I think I'm happier. It isn't so fast a
livin.

                         Like tomorrow, if I don't want to do anything, I won't set those
beans or whatever. I don't have to do it. And when I was workin, what made me so mad
when I worked: I'd have to work a whole day for the government, or more, and that
bothered me—to think I had to take orders from somebody else and listen to em and do
things wrong and get the devil for it, and still, you know, have to put up with that mess.
And he felt the same way. I mean, he worked for about twenty years in shops, and this
is another reason he went into the business: right in December when you needed work,
they'd lay you off, so you had nothing in the winter. So I think we're better off this way.
Of course, we don't have no big incomes, but we get by.

                         Sometimes it seems like we got help, when we really need it, you
know. It's not that we're religious—we're not religious.

ERIC: No. We believe, but we don't go overboard.

SARA: We don't go to church every Sunday.

ERIC: We don't go to church atall.

SARA: I used to go sometimes. But, ah, there is something. There is something that's guidin you somewheres along the line. Definitely. And that we define as God. A lot of it is inside yourself, but there is also something from the outside somewhere. I truly believe. But there's got to be something inside of you, too. To receive it. There's somebody that help. We say there's somebody up there helpin us. And I've seen it happen so many times: we, perhaps, sometimes we git right down but we don't know where we're gonna get another dollar from. And all of a sudden something happen. It comes. Not much, but enough to get you by.

And I can tell you one story: he was sick, not able to work. I was workin. And I do like to go to the races. And I've always done very good at the races. So it was in the spring. Somebody had given me some free passes for Suffolks. So my girl friend and I always went. So she said, "Let's go."

There he is home sick. And I left him lyin—he's cryin he don't know what he's gonna do. He's down on his back, and he didn't want me to go to begin with.

So we were jokin. We said to him, "Oh, we'll bring you back a bundle, and you'll be all happy."

So we took off. And we hit the double. Fine. We didn't make much on that. So we took and reinvested in what we call the twin double. That's hittin four races completely in a row. We hit it! I brought home fifteen hundred dollars that night. Fifteen one-hundred-dollar bills.

ERIC: If you don't think that there's something up over the ceilin—that would never, ever happen. You don't know me. But it never'd ever happen to me again in another thousand years. If I lived a thousand times. Never. With me flat on my back and have somethin come like that to help me over the hump, as bad off as I was, with kids to feed and kids to go to school. You don't think the Lord don't provide sometimes. You just want to try it sometimes. I really believe that He does.

SARA: I studied astrology quite a bit, and I feel the bad things that happen to us, there is a lesson tryin to be taught to us. Somebody—there's certain—I can't explain what it is. But of course, Satan is our lesson-teacher. He gives us our hardships, our really hard rubs in life, our fate. And I feel he tries to teach us if we don't live correctly on this earth and do right and live properly and love thy neighbor and be good to everybody, that we're apt to have to live this life over again.

To me it would be a punishment, in certain phases of it. I feel, of course, I've read a lot of those way-out books, and I think about it, and sometimes I believe it, and sometimes I can't accept it—that we have lived before. And I can't help but thinkin the crosses that I've had to bear in all my life—did I do something wrong in my other life that I lived, if I did live a life?

But I take that all with a grain of salt, you know. Mix it in with everything else and see if I can come up with something.

So many people say they couldn't stand to live out here. They couldn't stand it because there wouldn't be any noise like in the city.

ERIC: You lose your energy and you lose your power with the noise. You get tired quicker. And of course, when you're younger, you revitalize right back up again. I'm fifty-five now, and I feel that when you're young you come right back quick, but when you're older, you don't.

Tell me, what in the devil is the city people gonna do, figure what's gonna happen with the population growin and all. Are they gonna come out here and stomp on us and dig all our cabbage out of the cellar and throw us out into the street and grab what we've got and survive off'n it or what? Now that's what bothers me.

This is why I don't want to go back to the cities or ever see them again really. Because I'm kinda thinkin that might be what happen. Of course, if I got enough money to buy gun shells enough to fight em off—but you can't fight em off forever. You've got to start usin a fork or somethin to push em out of your way.

Like the law of the farm. If you took two hundred chickens and you put em in a house where there was only supposed to be one hundred, the next mornin you went down to feed the chickens, half of them would be gone. Because they'd git pickin em until they died—they'd git pickin their rear end until they bleed to death. They pick that boil in the back of the feathers, you know, on the backsides, you know. Chicken is made with the boil there to keep his feathers oiled. So they pick away at that thing until he dies, until he bleeds to death. Same thing, same law of averages is happenin with people in cities, where they're overcrowded.

There's some of my generation that still knows how to farm, but my kids and their offspring and their ones that they've married, they don't know nothing about it, see. And they ask me questions about it all the time, as to how you raise stuff, see. Well, all right. But would it be in time to take some of those people that come from the city—could you teach em fast enough? Would they hang onto the end of a hoe and hoe a row of corn, or would they just give up and go down to the brook and jump in? What would they do? That's what I'm wonderin.

They don't think about depressions, though. No. Because I've run across ones before and talked like this to him—he's all dressed up, he's about thirty-five, forty years old, he's in big business, he's in the bankin business, and he's never seen a depression, and I say to him, "Well, sometime, somehow this thing is gonna happen again."

He says, "Oh, no. No. They'll never let it happen again."

You wait and see. It won't be whether they let it happen again. It'll just happen, that's all. Something's gonna go off balance sometime, I think, because it did once, it will again, it can again. I won't say that it will, but it can.

And should it—well, we've got all the farm machinery that come off of the farm in Scarborough to go farmin again if we have to. Everything. Tractors, plows. Well, you saw em out there. And they aren't very handsome . . .

SARA: They're pretty rusty, but they still work.

ERIC: They're pretty rusty, but they still work.

Cape Meddick, Maine

Hephaestus was the Greek god who was considered too ugly to be the child of Truth (Hera) and Power (Zeus). So he was cast out of Olympus while still an infant, and fell into the sea, where beautiful nymphs took him and cared for him in their cave. When he grew older and knew the truth, he gained entry to Olympus and was revered for the beautiful things he made on his anvil and his forge.

You cannot see Russell Hayes' place from the road. You must drive a ways on gravel, then on dirt, through a thick wood. Then you see it. It looks like a shack set amidst an unconventional dump, but the closer one looks at the dump, the stranger, more mysterious, more threaded with something of the occult it becomes. Things are halved and stand on end. Metal pansies swing from a cast iron tree. Rain barrels, cut from water heaters, make bath tubs in the yard; here the front end of a thresher, there a spare tire.

The shack seems soft and squashed as it sits surrounded by dense forest, the sun coming through the greenery in thick, sharp blades, the yard around it cruel and wild, full of hard-edged contrast, sharp metal edges, cast iron things, heaped and sprawled across each other like a madman's dream, an artist's vision—Bergman, Fellini, Bunuel. As the sun rises higher in the sky, the shadows cast from the strange shapes in the yard become more primeval: huge oil drums recline crazily against each other. Over there the anvil, a huge generator, odds and ends, and amidst the rubble, like blossoms in a war-torn city, are budding flowers.

Russell Hayes is a welder. He stands at the top of the stairs outside his two-story shack; a thick, muscled man, his head is shaven, his eyes are blue and intense, his hands are calloused, his face is lined and creased. He sees we are with his friends, and we are welcome.

The first floor of the shack is his winter blacksmith's shop. The stairs lead to his second-floor living quarters, heralded by a sign, AMORAL HAUNT. There are two rooms on this floor, a kitchen and a study-bedroom. One is shocked at the blackness of the sheets; too black for dirt. And then I realize, carbon. One night when I see him I see how the carbon has blackened everything, seeming to seep even into the whites of his eyes. He would save the sheets, I think, if he washed at night, and he does wash. But he takes his bath in the morning in the rain barrel. He lives by the sun when he can and loves the play of light in the woods that surround the house. "En . . . lightened," he says slowly, and asks if I know what it means, really know what it means to be that. I think of the casual easiness of metaphor, and yet wonder at a man whose trade depends on looking at a fire so bright it blinds one without glasses.

He is a philosopher by nature and by trade, if one wishes to stay with metaphors. For inside the house, the fragments of the yard appear again in different forms: words and pictures clipped and hung, pasted sideways, halfways, upside down; sayings and bodies of nude women, mostly cut from *Playboy* magazine; and amidst the bodies, hanging from the ceiling, from fixtures, parts, parts of things inanimate—rubber tubes and springs and lightbulbs and sockets, hangers and extension cords; the playmate of the month; and a poster explaining The Facts of Life.

Russell Hayes speaks and thinks often in fragments: Plato, Omar Khayam, St. Augustine, interweaving always eternity, beauty, and sexuality. Metaphor again, but his role as a welder seems to be the way he thinks and confronts his own thinking to put together that which time, corrosion, rust, circumstance, accident, and passion has put asunder. His most striking characteristic is his intensity.

It is impossible to meet him in what would ordinarily be described as a casual way. One is touched by something permanent. One suspects that in this person is a place for endless attachments. Amidst the rubble, the fragmentation, the preoccupation with sexual attitudes and feelings, issue strange tandems. "Of course I'll take my clothes off. Is the human body something to be ashamed of?" Then, "Oh, she's a whore."

"A whore?" I say, a strange kind of judgement from a man who believes in amorality.

"Yes," he says, no contradiction, "she ran off and divorced her husband while he was at sea and married another man."

"Were you at sea?" I ask.

"Oh yes, a long time, years I was at sea." He shows me photographs.

This kind of moral judgement is not the strange incongruity it appears to be in a man who otherwise seems simply to want to understand and respond to people; it has less to do with whoring than with leaving. He has no tolerance for severed attachments. He is sixty-some years old and cannot speak of his mother (who died a few years ago) without being overwhelmed. Tears stream down the crease-lined face, mixing with threads of carbon lying there, a slow black issue falling from his cheeks, tears of sorrow and pain, a reminder that time does not, for most of us, alter our attachment; it just makes rationalizations easier. We learn to accept, perhaps.

Russell Hayes does not. He avoids sentiment and nostalgia and lives with the pain of loves lost as he lives with the wind. It blows through on some days so that you feel it a lot, and then you shiver and cry and let it blow.

He survives minimally on low-cost, canned food, using tin foil insulation in his shack. But these are not the things that sustain him. He survives really by a gift for friendship, by a huge outgoing rush of interest in sharing the things he knows, in sharing a sense of discovery and of connections. He wants to be and is a welder who attempts to join himself with his audience the way he joins things with his hands. He survives on this. Friendship gets him by. His friends are real and come often. His great pleasure is their company.

He works as much as he can, sometimes into the night. In the winter he runs for road commissioner, so that the publicity will remind people in the area that there is a welder nearby. He has done many different odd-job things in his life, worked at building tunnels, spent time at sea, took photographs for a newspaper. His life has been full of odds and ends, which is the way most lives may be; his incongruities just seem more sharply distinguished.

He has owned a little land and sold most of it off a piece at a time to friends. He wants to be surrounded by thoughts of the philosophers, friends, the woods, sunlight, and a welder's work. That is what he has.

Russell Hayes

I've lived here nine years. Well, you see, my father is ninety-three years old this year, last June. And my mother died just at Christmas time, but she was off her feet pretty much, and she was a—what do you say?—diabetic. So I had to be here. She was a diabetic, and I would take her out, you know what I mean, and so forth. So I spent the last nine years taking care of my mother. Now I'm free. Mother is dead; father isn't well. Don't you see? But now my father, of course, is still living, but he's no better off. People become—that point where they don't think too much—senile. Yes.

My cousin, I call her a prostitute for the simple reason she is. Well, her husband was away at sea. He was the chief mate on my ship. I was captain of a tugboat, and I took him on as chief mate, because he didn't have a job. And while he was in the South Pacific with me, she divorced him and took on another man and sold the house and bought a new car. Know what I mean?

"Sex is one of the kindest things two people can do for each other." Of course, that's a quote by somebody. If I like it, I write it down so I'll remember it. And then when I want to recall it, I don't recall it the moment I want to sometimes. Sex is all you live for. Man is put on this earth to impregnate every woman he meets. That is his ultimate motive. Woman wants security, so she wants to get one and pin him, imprison him.

I don't think marriage is a good idea. No. No, I don't. I think living together is a good idea, but not marriage. Because there you lose your independence. Your lose your independence because then the state takes over. And the state tells you what you can do and what you cannot do. Right? And they do it so effectively.

You're living in an age that is becoming a little freer than we had before when I was being brought up. I was not allowed to look—as a child growing up, as a boy—at a clothes line with women's clothes on it. You imagine that? I was not allowed to see the pages of women's clothes in the Sears Roebuck catalog.

It's like being forced to go to Sunday school until you're old enough so you can be independent. And then you say, "The hell with it. They've lied to me." Throw it completely off. Become unbrainwashed.

This is all brainwash. This country is brainwashed. Every person in it. You're brainwashed from the first day you go to school. You repeat the salute to the flag, and you used to have a little prayer—it didn't mean a thing, you know what I mean? But now I wouldn't dare fly an American flag out there.

I'm flying a flag, the flag of truce. That's what that white flag means. I put it out white. Then I decided we're not only quitting, but we're yellow, pulling out of Vietnam and everything. So I got a piece of yellow flag out there. But the yellow one turned white. You know what I mean? So maybe that's the way it is.

You've heard of man's inhumanity to man, haven't you? But did you ever think of God's inhumanity to man? Well, think of it once in a while. Do I believe in God? Course . . . not. God is a word just like chair. Could be any kind of a chair. God is something to pray to or something? No. God is all around us. If you want the word God, God is the universe. There is no good in it, and there is no bad in it. It is there. It is just your opinion, you know. If you think something's bad, it's bad to you. That doesn't mean it's bad, does it?

Things go independently of whatever people think. Morals? What are you talkin about morals? Did you see that sign out there? It says amoral, a-m-o-r-a-l, haunt, h-a-u-n-t. Where you are right now. Amoral Haunt. Now, amoral means not concerned with morals. Now, let's look at it this way: if morals are religious scruples, right, now in the Jewish religion—I shouldn't mention the religion—but if somebody has to have the end of his cock cut off to stay with that church or his scruples, then I say the hell with it. If somebody Catholic—I've mentioned one religion, we'll mention em all—has to have his hair shaved off, or rather, her hair shaved off and wear something all the time to cover her head—and that not only takes place in the Catholic Church, it also does in the Jewish. You know, the Jews fight among themselves as much as the other religions fight

among themselves, because they've got so many sects. In other words, Christianity happens to be wonderful.

Now my hair's shaved off, cause I work under a welding helmet, and it's more comfortable. And hair, being the dirtiest thing on your body, catches more dirt than anything else. I don't want it. I even shave my chest. Why sure. I understand women like to have that hair rub against them in bed or something, but somehow I think I don't feel through the hair. I would rather have it shaved off and be closer, you see. Pubic hair, yes, whenever I have time. If possible.

But I don't do any laundry. See those overalls, the ones I'll put on when I go out to work? This is my trademark: my overalls. People don't see these around here, because they're steelworkers' overalls. But in my trade, everybody wears these. I wear em till I burn em out. Usually burn em out before I wear em out. The dirt and grease and grime is mine or off an old car or something. It isn't going to infect me in any way. I'm not afraid of my own dirt. I'm not afraid of the dirt off a truck or a bulldozer. I might be afraid of screwing some girl, afraid of venereal disease. I would be very afraid, yes. I'd be very particular. In fact I've been that way all my life.

Workin out there all day, I get pretty goddamned dirty, I'll tell you. What I usually do is I wash in my rain barrel. Well, I go out there and wash in it.

I feel most comfortable bare-assed. I'm always runnin around this house bare-assed. The first thing I do when I get in this house is shed my clothes.

Now, you take this welding business. I took up welding before the Second World War, because I didn't want to join the Army. I wanted to be a specialist, and I became a specialist. I became a pot-boiler in Todd's Shipyard. Then I had a chance to go to Officers' Training School. And I had one hell of a job to get out of the shipyard in order to go to school. When I went to school I had to make a grade of ninety. If I didn't make a grade of ninety every month, I was chucked out. I was out, completely out; then I was A-1 in the Army.

So I stayed up to study, and they called me Sleepy, because I was so sleepy in the daytime when I went to class, because I was up all night studying in order to get that grade of ninety. You see what I mean? And I made it.

I was commissioned by the United States Congress as an Ensign. And

I said, "I'll never do this again." And like a goddamned fool, I went back, and came out as a Lieutenant JG.

After that, well, I sailed oil tankers. I was second mate on the second largest oil tanker in the world in 1950. But you got an oil tanker, and you're up there on the bridge, and you got charge for four hours there—you have charge eight hours a day, but I mean four-hour shifts. And that tanker is moving, and it's moving in such a way— about eighteen knots or something—and if a fisherman decides to cross your path or some goddamned coast guard boat that don't know where he's going—the coast guard don't know shit about navigation—you know you can't stop, you can't stop before they arrive. And if they do not follow the rules of the road, you're licked, see. You're going to hit em for sure if they don't get out of the way.

But another thing about the rules of the road is they do have to follow that rule until collision is inevitable. When collision is inevitable, then you try to avoid it. When collision is *inevitable,* then you're allowed to try to avoid it. If it's inevitable, how the hell are you going to avoid it? Well, that's the rules of the road.

When I come home, I got married. Oh, I got married twice. First time, I came from sea, and I came to a party, see, at Betty Brevhegney's home. And they were so destitute—there was her and her mother living alone—and they were so destitute, and the farm was about to be taken away from them. And she told me what the doctor had said: to get herself a boy friend. And she wasn't too well, because she had just been released from a hospital for tuberculosis, TB hospital. And the poor little thing couldn't get the house painted, couldn't get this and that done. And I was just released from the service, so I says, "Well, I'll come down and help you." And that's the way it started.

I married her to take care of her. Then I found that in order to pay the bills I had to return to sea, cause I could make six hundred dollars a month at sea clear to help pay the bills. Happened to be in New York when she died.

Then for three years I had to take care of her mother, who was about eighty-four when she died, I believe. And she was an alcoholic, and had fifty dollars a month pension and was very difficult to handle at times, because she spent all her money on liquor.

And the second time was, why, the girl said I knocked her up, that I impregnated her, whatever you call it, you know. I should have taken her to a doctor, but I didn't. And I found out it was just one of those—she wasn't pregnant. She just tried to take everything I had, that was all. And well, a gentleman would marry a woman if she said she was pregnant, wouldn't he? Well, I was a gentleman. It lasted about five months, I think, until I found out what the story was.

I live here in the woods because I own the land, for one thing. From my first wife. Well, I started out with about a hundred and twenty acres, and now I've got about four acres, because I've picked out the nicest people and sell it to them. I mean artists and gentlemen. Really nice people.

I built this house. Build it. It's not built yet. Well, you see, I've got my ladder to the roof from the porch. I'm gonna put a nice little picket fence around there, or probably, I'd like to put ironwork if I can. You see, that's my trade. And then up there, I can go up there and sun and have flower boxes and things. I love flower boxes.

This is built as no other house. Other houses have a hangover on the front or the back, but nobody ever builds a house with a hangover on four sides. My hangover's about eighteen inches on the three sides, and I think, about two feet on the front. The front is towards my primeval, little grove out there of pine trees, and I call that my primeval. I didn't want to head it to the road, because I like to watch the race of men go by, you see, but I don't particularly want to watch a race of idiots go by. And I didn't put in any big show window, because when I'm in my house, I like to be by myself. I don't want people looking at me. And you notice all these big windows they put in their front room. As you go by, you can see everything that's going on in there. I don't know why they do it.

In the winter, those overhangs are filled with sawdust. Now, if sawdust can keep ice all summer in an ice house, it can keep me warm in the winter. There's anything that will keep something cold, will also keep something warm. Now this house is finished off with—what do you call this cardboard that they make boxes out of?—corrugated cardboard. The air space's in there. Now in college I learned that an air space, if it was only ten one-thousandths of an inch thick, is efficient as one that is an inch thick, like between your storm windows. So if you put two sheets of glass in here, with a slip of paper around to separate em ten one-thousandths of an inch, it'd be just equal to a storm window. But you would have to seal em so you wouldn't have to clean em on the inside.

On this stove: any stove takes the air out of the room to burn, takes so much air. What creates fire, of course you know: first you have to have something that will burn, then you have to have the heat of combustion, and then you have to have oxygen to make it burn. Without oxygen you don't have any fire.

Well, the air that goes through this stove is what allows this oil to burn. This air has to be taken out of the room. And air has to come in from the outside to replace it. So it is coming under the cracks in the doors and through the windows. By putting that pipe down through the floor, I am feeding the cold air to the burner, so the heat from the outside of the stove just reheats the air that is in the room. There's no air coming in here under the doors. It reheats the air that is present. The air that is going up the chimney is coming from downstairs in the shop downstairs. The cold air is what is feeding the burner, see, to make it burn. Got to have air to burn. And then it's going up that chimney. So we reheat the air that's here. We're not heating new, cold air that's coming in, that's ten below zero or something like that. You know, if you had a fireplace and a real tight house, you couldn't burn that fireplace unless you cracked the door a little bit for enough air to come in to go up the chimney.

I do all my own cooking. As I said, I worked two summers as a baker in a one-man bake shop. Show you how to make bread some time. Doughnuts, cream puffs, puff paste. You know how to roll em? I think you roll it to about one hundred forty-eight layers or something.

I eat out of a lot of cans. Once in a while I like a real raw potato to peel and cook, because as a child I was brought up on em. And I love to cook pea soup. Season it the way I want to, and have crackers in the soup. Night before last, I had oyster stew. I love that. I get the oysters in a can and put milk with em and season it to my taste.

Now I live here alone and I work. Oh, people call me over for the nastiest old—they bring me cast iron and stuff like that. It's foolish to try to weld it, but you've got to try to help people, see. Lots of times I'll put three hours in, and I'll

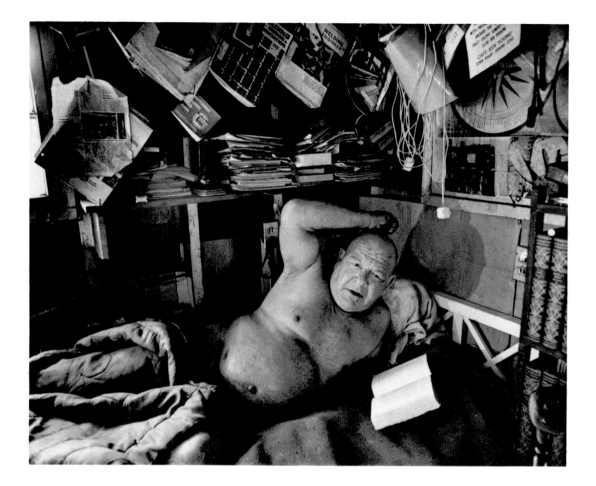

charge one hour on an old piece of equipment, because, well, they can't afford it. The equipment isn't worth it. What are you gonna do?

A guy come in here yesterday, and I did a job for him. And actually it was about six dollars. He said, "I'll be right back to pay you." He gave me one dollar and "be right back to pay you."

So I said, "Leave me your spare tire." Know what I mean? I'm just getting smart. "Leave me your spare tire." So the spare tire is out there, and until I get the five dollars, he won't have it.

Canyon, California

In the hills of Berkeley, outside of San Francisco, there is a beautiful territory of lush redwood forests, running brooks, and soft hills covered with green. One is awed by the perfection of it. I turn onto a dirt road, which forks into another dirt road, some parts of which are paved. Some of the houses are elegant, good-looking country homes. At the top of one rise, however, another phenomenon greets the eye: there is a house without sides. It is quite beautiful, with a roof of eucalyptus poles and a sturdy flooring, almost circular. Around the house the eucalyptus trees bend and sway in the wind. In the center of the floor is a fireplace. Almonds are roasting in a tin can on the fire, and I am offered some when I arrive unexpectedly to explain my visit.

Harry James is the name of the young man who lives in this house, which he designed, with a young woman named Nancy. They have been living in it for three years. I am invited to go down to the second floor, where it might be warmer, for it is cold for California today—thirty-seven degrees. It is not much warmer on the second floor, which is walled on one side by the hill into which the house is built, and is an open half circle on the other, which faces out into the eucalyptus trees. One arc of the circle, about five feet wide, is enclosed with a pane of glass. In front of this is a mattress. There is a bath tub, which faces the trees. The tub, Harry explains, is cast iron, and the water they pour into it is heated by building a fire in the stones underneath.

When I go back upstairs, there is a rooster wandering through the living room, and Nancy has moved to the side to attend to the goats.

When I ask why they have goats, Harry smiles and shrugs, "I don't know why I have them. I just have them."

Although Harry is very concerned with changing structures and changing living habits and attitudes, some of the other people I meet in Canyon seem to consider the verbal approach to anything, most particularly the question of why, an absurd convention. It is difficult to know how much this comes out of philosophy and how much it comes from an uneasiness about the tape recorder. Some of these other persons live in what appear to be wooden wigwams, made totally out of scrap wood and shingles. I do not see any familiar shape, or even any geodesic domes. Although the houses appear to be slipshod because they are irregular—some of them look like igloos and soccer balls—they have been highly praised by the professors at the University of California's School of Environmental Design.

In a small trailer, overlooking a valley, I meet a young man, who says his name is Carl. He is painting a design on the back of a leather jacket, and as he does this he explains how many people living in Canyon live off the surplus of the country. Another friend comes in and explains that nobody in Canyon is poor. They live well on food stamps. The accessibility to cities here makes all the difference in their living conditions. If Willoby's well water were to be contaminated, Willoby would be in trouble. When the sewage got into the drinking water in Canyon, Carl went to the local gas station and filled up jugs with water. When he needs extra money for something other than food, he goes out and chops firewood. The attitude seems to be: don't worry, you're not going to starve to death; California is a rich place. And compared to Maine, it's a warm place, although some of the people in the huts, and certainly Carl, are physically uncomfortable. In the trailer, there was no heat available save body heat.

Extra food is gotten by some people in this community from the throwaways behind large supermarkets. It is that that has caused such activity to be labeled "garbage culture." But it is really "surplus culture," a commitment to using what is considered waste by a wealthy society in order not to waste it, an attitude that seems especially suited to the abundances of California.

Harry James

Well, you could actually, if we had to, live on no money for quite a while. We have. You know, a lotta times. Because you don't pay rent, the water comes out of the ground, because it's a very rich area, brimming over with garbage, an a lot of it's usable. Lot of it's edible.

There was a little kinda prefab cabin here before, an I started fixin it up, building around it, which was a good front, you know. It got me past the building department for quite a while. The poles, they're eucalyptus poles. They grow like bamboo around here. It's a very common material, overlooked by most people, because, ah well, the building techniques were developed before eucalyptus was introduced in this country, you know. It's very available and pretty useful in this form, which is like poles, you know. You jus go an cut em, you know. Then you strip em, take the bark off.

We get limited protection from the rain. Like upstairs here in a heavy rainstorm gets pretty wet. Although in a light rain, don't get wet at all.

Downstairs is our bedroom, also a bath an shower. That's gonna be the loft over there.

This house is based on something that I've seen pictures of in Mexico. The idea of hyperbolic paraboloid is something that's been used in the last, well—I guess Gaudi was using it in Spain. Incandela is using it in thin-shell concrete form in Mexico. This particular arrangement, though, I've never seen before. An also, making it out of wood, eucalyptus poles. I've seen it done with, ah, with wood, but not this way.

Fireplace, that's a piece of culvert. I guess you call it a sleeve or a collar when you have two big pieces of culvert pipe and they meet end to end and they put this other piece around an join em. Galvanized steel. And it's got three layers of fire brick underneath it.

This is such a rich area—you have to learn to see it, I guess—but you need some kinda materials, this is a very good area to be, because you can find it layin around somewhere, you know. There's an awful lot of building going on in this area. Like I grew up around here an I've seen it—incredible population explosion. And so that means an awful lot of building an stuff. And the West Coast is very rich in timber, wood. It's just everywhere, you know. An if you can find ways to use it—for example, there's telephone poles, railroad ties, you know, bridge timbers, all kinds of gross materials that aren't very popular with anybody. And it's very easy to develop building techniques that can use that kind of stuff, cause it's good material.

What it boils down to is you go to building sites and get a whole lot of short pieces, for example, and if you get into geodesic domes and things, you can find ways of spanning great distances with short pieces. If you have a lot of the same of something, which is like an industrial spin-off or something, you might find a big pile of something you could use, and there's ways of putting those things together now. That's what's happened in building in this century, you know, is ways of putting a lot of little things together, stuff like that, you know, you can span a lotta distance.

This place is like, um, you know, it's not far from the city. For me it's too close to it, you know. Like I'm tryin to maintain some kind of illusion about this being the country. But anyway, practically speaking, it means that we have all these things around that we can get. Like any kind of fuel or any kind of material. It's right here, you know. Like everything comes in from all over the world in San Francisco port over there. An everything's around. You can get cheap things from Japan, you need stuff like that. And then California, for instance, all this tremendous produce an agriculture an everything, so you can get all that stuff really cheap, too, just organize your stuff a little bit. And it's just so easy, you know, that it makes the whole thing seem like a game—not serious, you know. But, ah, I like it.

Carl

We're living without even land. When you have land, when you can afford to rent or something or have a piece of property, you always have something, you know, something which you can do something with. But like Harry, he's got quite a bit: not only does he own land, but like he controls all the land up here. You know, just, he's boss up here. So he gets a lotta things that he wants. He's got a lot of people—he talks—he's a very good speaker, you know. He's very easy to understand, nice to talk to. He gets turned onto a lotta stuff, a lotta jobs and stuff. I never seen Harry really try to work. We all work when we have to.

Nancy works. A teacher. His ole lady. She works at the child-care center. We still live off the garbage a lot. Not lately though, even since she's been a teacher. She brings, you know, a lotta stuff home from child-care center to eat.

See, the garbage, it's really not like garbage. It's really pretty decent vegetables an stuff. Get it in the back where they throw it out, the Safeway garbage, you know, big industrial market garbage. Like they throw out all the overripe fruit an stuff an vegetables. An really, well, it's just good anyway. You know, dented cans, and eggs and like cottage cheese has to go after a certain time. So it's out there every week. Ice cream. Margarine. Anything that spoils. An they got—the state sets a certain date that they can hold certain merchandise. An after that they have to throw it away, you know. So. It's aroun. We live off it for a very long time.

This is my friend's trailer. He's pretty lucky. He's really got a good thing up here. He's got propane, an he's got refrigerator, stove. That's a hell of a lot more'n I've had for a long time. You know, like this is really groovy. I can sit down'n do my thing here.

Actually, you wanna live subsistently, the first thing you're gonna do is take what you're used to living in an cut it at least ten times to the size you can keep it warm. Otherwise, like you can't maintain a place subsistent living unless it's the right size, you know, for you to survive in. Like you'll find that Fred started with a real big house. The next house he got smaller. And now he's down to a little bitty house. That's because he realizes that you can't heat a big house. Alls you can really do is with your own body temperature heat a very small place. And that's with really adequate insulation, really adequate building, really adequate insulation.

W hen I was younger, I used to come out here an fool around, you know, an get stoned with the kids, like everybody did. And, ah, as I grew older, I got friends, like Harry and Michael Fox an some other people: Fred, Bruce, lotta people. And I started to take, you know, living out here seriously, because there was a lotta problems that I thought I could help people in the community with. And like there's always something to do. So.

Like workin in the water project, you know. We gotta get all our own water outta the spring. We don't have any public facilities, because the state MUD, that's the state water department, won't give us any. So anyway, we gotta dig our own well an all, an spring, an get our own pump, an pump the water up the hill. We gotta take care of our own elimination, build septic tanks an all that. Stuff that most people aren't used to. An like there's about eleven people on our own water system, an it's really bad. Like if there's just one person on one well, I can see that. But like the way it is now, there's so many people on the water system, that makes it really tough.

Well, anyway, getting back to how I moved here: I was doing some work around there, and then I got sick. So I went into a mental hospital. An like I remember in the mental hospital, all I could remember was looking out the window an thinking about Canyon, you know. An like I couldn't stand it there. It was jus driving me nuts. So I split. Placed every thought, you know, about going back to Canyon. So when I got out of the mental institution, I worked for about six months, I guess, an then I jus came out here an stayed.

Just living. You know. I don't have any money to buy any land. What I did at first: I knew Michael Fox, and I asked Michael if I could stay there until

I got my shit together, at his house. And he said yeah. An I stayed there for about four months, then moved outta there. An then I was up on the hill there for a while.

The house I'm sposed to live in now, I'm not living in, cause there's another guy there, an me an him don't get along so well. So he's gonna build his house downstairs from me. An I kinda told him I'd let him do it, so he's brought all the lumber up there. So I can't really tell him he can't do it. I don't have any right to tell anybody what they can or can't do up here anyway. So I'm jus lettin him do his thing and build the downstairs so he can get the hell outta the upstairs. He's wreckin the upstairs for me.

The house, Fred built it. Fred Heathcock. It's a really excellent structure. It's just, the guys that was living there before, Bruce an Betsy, did some crazy things like putting papier mâché on the roof. An that's why it looks so terrible now, since all the roof fell apart an everything. It came down an made a big mess. And it was all wet an everything. Bruce an Betsy were jus living there for the summer, so therefore they jus, you know, did a groovy art trip on the roof. When I first move in there, I was just drenched about three days straight. I went an got a big piece a plastic an put it over the roof, an it stopped leakin. But it's still a mess.

It's a hyperbolic paraboloid. It's partially a hyperbolic paraboloid, an then some of the structure's reversed. I don't even know what hyperbolic paraboloid is. That's what Fred told me it is. It's built on triangles. The whole basis of the building is triangles. Not really triangles, pyramids. It's very hard to explain. You'll have to ask Fred. It's got a foundation an everything. That house's a very together house. Like there's people up here living in teepees an everything, but that house—none of Fred's houses are on the line of a teepee. Actually they're almost impossible to take down. Wood structure foundation. Wood stove. An you cut your wood. Runnin out aroun here, too. For light, I got a couple lanterns. I got a lotta candles. A friend of mine works in a candlestick factory, gives me candles. Matter of fact, they live right down the hill.

We eat pretty nourishin food. Lotta grains, meat. Eat about just about normal things, you know, except, ah, there's not much of it. For money I get food stamps. That's about it. Really. Always have enough to buy a beer once in a while.

I'm learning how to paint on leather; never done it before. Tryin all these little things. I used to just paint, like an artist-type trip. But lately I've, ah, got into making stencils, which are more fun, I think.

57.

Take a look what I use. Like everything I use, everything there is just junk. There isn't any professional equipment, cept for the shoe dye there, you know, boot polish. An the other things are those little marking pens.

If I need something, I go out an get it. Depends how I get it. Might be an odd job. What I'd like to do is start selling my art work.

State takes care a you when you're sick. Go down to Martinez. There's a lotta bacteria in the water that people aren't used to, cause, you know, we do our own filtration an everything. So. Subsequently, you get sick pretty easily when you first come up here.

Right now I get my water out of a service station. This trailer is outta water, an I don't know how to put the water in there. Live here till Monday when Bruce comes back.

There's an outhouse we use for local sanitation. Put it that way. It's not legal. But it's there. Better'n nothing. Really better'n nothing. It's a hole in the ground, you know, one of them.

Clothes? We make em. Well, you know, like don't make everything, but I put em all together. Use old clothes. It's no good making rags outta clothes, so, clothes outta rags.

Daufuskie Island, South Carolina

"You go down there on the river, front of the Boar's Head Tavern, go bout ten yars up the beach. That's the boat to Fuskie. Only goes twice a week." He scratches his head, our plaid-shirted informant, and looks at us with a squint. "You goin there?"

We nod.

"Ain't no white people there. Sure you goin there?"

We nod.

"Where you goin stay? Ain't nothin on Fuskie. I mean nothin."

"Some people are expecting us."

"Oh."

Our informant executes a three-yard spit, turns away, and shuffles to the end of the road. We are standing on a small street just off the square of elegant, old Savannah, full of mansions and Spanish moss, trying to find the boat that will take us to Daufuskie Island, a sea island miles down the Savannah River, where it runs into the sea.

The steam-driven motor launch resembles the famed, old war-horse, The African Queen—its size, its shape, its noise. The captain watches us, talking rapidly in a kind of singsong lilt, that suggests something of a West Indian accent, but is very different. He and his helper, a strong, heavily muscled, young, black man in a green tee shirt and a cap, unload the boat, tied to a small, rickety, old pier on the Savannah River. It is a hot day for March. There is not much to unload from the boat: a couple of cans for refilling gasoline and a small sack of mail. This boat is the mail boat, the grocery boat, and the passenger vessel to Daufuskie. It only goes to Savannah twice a week, and once a week to Beaufort, South Carolina. The passengers today are black ladies in pretty summer frocks, and one or two pipe-smoking gentlemen. There is an air of summertime and the South about the scene as the wind flicks the dresses, blue and pink and yellow, and hands raise to hats to contain the breeze. A shy, skinny girl stands near me, wiggling back and forth on one foot when I talk to her. She is seventeen and has just finished high school. She was born on Daufuskie and lived there until she finished junior high school. There is only one schoolhouse on the island and one teacher. To go to high school, she had to live with relatives in Savannah. She has decided to stay and try to find work. This day she is "seein my aunt to the boat." When I ask her about Fuskie she shrugs, "Nothin to do on Fuskie. Everybody gettin old." Then she spins, her sandals flying, and runs up the street.

A black, middle-aged woman, a former schoolteacher, born on Daufuskie, settles down next to me in the boat. Cissy Frank has lived all her life on the island and lives there now with some chickens, "cause they're somethin to care for," and pigs, because they're something to eat. She works as a family health aide on the island, which she talks about with nostalgia and pride.

It is about a two-hour ride down the river, then a turn into some marshland, just before the ocean. It is about a half-hour ride through salt water marshes, until the island is pointed out to me. It is a still, small island, offering Spanish moss, sand roads, romantic impressions, and an occasional alligator.

There are one or two old jalopies on the island, circa 1940, which are waiting for the boat. They are used to haul groceries and anything heavy to whoever ordered it from the mainland. A few children are playing around the pier as we dock, and a tough old lady, who is eighty-some years old, I am told, is striding toward the dock at a quick pace, waving her cane in the air. The captain says she has walked the half mile to the pier and will walk it back faster than any of us can do it. She has come to meet her relatives, who are staying with her for a week. They are from New York City, and when we meet them a few days later, they are grumbling about having nothing to do.

There isn't much to do. You can walk the island end to end in about an hour, and the width in about forty-five minutes, seeing nothing but trees and moss and an occasional house. If you go near the swamps, you might see an alligator. The houses are small and simple. Some are rebuilt, former slave cabins. The island was once a plantation, and some of the parents of the current inhabitants and some grandparents received land when the plantation collapsed. The house we are staying in is a low-ceilinged home with five rooms, a back porch that has been boarded up to make an extra room, and a front porch. Hogs are wandering about the yard as we walk up.

The largest room is the parlor, which is decorated with two satin pillows and many doilies. The sofa is worn, as is the highly polished glass coffee table. There are ashtrays and small vases scattered about. It is used only on very special occasions. The other rooms include a kitchen, which has a gas stove, a dining room, and the closed-in porch with a wood stove. Mrs. Arlington likes to cook on the wood stove, and when we have gone to bed, she and Mr. Arlington will sit and talk in front of it for hours.

Mr. and Mrs. Arlington will sleep in their bedroom with their nephew, about nine years old, the few days we, the guests, stay there.

Pollution has killed off the oyster business, and there has been no work available to Daufuskie people for over two years. Mr. and Mrs. Arlington live on less than twenty-five dollars a week, which is what their social security payments are. It is almost impossible to see how they survive on this. They have a television set, which they are careful to run only about an hour in the evening, and electric lights, which are also carefully watched. I would guess the lights are on about an hour a day. There is an old freezer, a necessity when the shopping can only be done once a month. The monthly electric bill comes to the astonishing sum of eighteen dollars, which leaves about twenty dollars a week for everything, including hog feed.

"It costs," Mrs. Arlington says, shaking her head, "it costs to feed a pig." As it is, they eat a lot of grits.

We, as the guests, are given bacon for breakfast and dinner, along with grits and milk and doughnuts. Mrs. Arlington goes to a great deal of trouble to fix our meals and makes a wonderful okra and tomato mixture one night. The table is set with a cloth and a centerpiece of small plastic flowers in a vase. The floors are washed so they sparkle. I wonder, since I know wax would be a luxury, and she smiles and says she just mops it a lot. The Arlingtons do not join us for meals. When invited, they protest they are not hungry or they have already eaten. They are full of pride and strength and anger. Mrs. Arlington knows it will soon be impossible to live on what she gets as social security.

On the way to the boat, at the end of our stay, as Mr. Arlington moves through the pine forests with us, helping with our bags, moving with a speed and litheness of a man a third his age, smiling and saying "It was a real pleasure to meet youall," one feels he means it. There is a curious exuberance of spirit among the people I have met, especially the old people, that I find hard to understand. Although discouraged, they are not defeated.

Mr. Arlington works all day, feeding hogs, which run about, helping fix the cars, which break down, mending fences, raking the grounds, planting and tending. Mrs. Arlington nourishes the community, her husband, her daughter who lives down the road, her grandchildren. Bone tired and with no hope of increased income in inflationary times, she has a strength far beyond stiff-upper-lip determination. It wells up inside from some place I can't discover. Her "leg painin," she seems enriched and enviable as she sits and rocks, singing spirituals in a full, joyous voice, singing with a lilt and strength and sadness, praising God.

Flossie Arlington

It's a whole lotta people die that lived here. They die. Whole lotta people die. And it's a whole lot leave from here and end up in the city, cause it wasn't no work. They didn't have anything to do, no way. They have to leave from here to make a living. Nothin for them to do.

The government give them a little help, but not much. I'm gonna tell you straight: the government gives a little, but they don't give enough. They say they gonna raise it, but you gotta see that first. Now, they give me a little social security. Well, that ain't nothin much, cause, you know, I can't live off thirty-eight dollars and fifty cents. That's what they give me a month. And I got the pig and I gotta buy groceries. I got to pay a light bill and I got to pay pharmacy. I don't have nothin.

Joe gets some by himself. Give him fifty-three. And he ain't done a lick a work now two years. I go right ahead and live off the stamp a little bit and try to save em and clean this buildin and everything, buy a little food. I get twenty-eight fifty. Time I go to Savannah and I pick up a buggy and I goes round, I got thirty dollars or thirty-five or forty dollars in the buggy.

See, I planted a little garden. I raise a little butterbeans, okra, tomatoes, green peas, and corn. I made a lotta okra, and I secure my okra. What I do with it: I jus cut it up and fix it decent and put it in the freezer. Plant a little potatoes, sweet potatoes, but I didn't make no sweet potatoes this season on account of we have a flood: rain, the water settles, they wouldn't dig the ditch—all the ditch need diggin out—the water come all over the fields, all the potato's rotten. Hard over here.

And pig, well, you got to feed a hog, you know. You got to buy feed.

You got to buy hog feed; you got to buy corn. You got to buy corn feed the chickens and everything. If you don't make it, you still got to feed it, but when I make it, I feed the hog with it.

No way here. That's why so many people leave from here. Oh, I tell you, they scatter all about. They leave from here cause they couldn't stay here, no job.

I'll leave here one of these days when the good Lord calls me from here. I'm gonna get ready to go when the good Lord calls me. Nowhere to go now. Stay home now.

The tenth of June, I'll be seventy-four. I feel good. I'm gonna tell you, I feel good. But see, sometimes my leg, it's poor in the cold. See, one time back we used to open oysters. And it was cold on the shore. And I catch cold in my legs.

Yeah, they had a factory right down the dock. But nobody don't buy oysters now. People jus up and gone. They said pollution. They oysters done died.

Still, we got lovely beach on this island. Lots of white folk come here and go on the beach. Every man come in their own boat. Big, beautiful speedboats. Sometimes they'll have thirty boats on that beach.

Water we get from the pump. The government—we suppose to get it, we suppose to have runnin water, but I don't know. I guess when it comes here, my Master done called me from here. We suppose to get it. I believe. I tell you the truth: I sure wish we could get that. If we could get this runnin water and get any work on the island, it'd be so much that folks come back home to live. There's so many people leave from here on account of they couldn't make a living. You would leave, too, you can't get money to live off. You can't make money to live off, before you get hungry, see, it'd make you steal.

Cissy Frank

I don't think I would be here on the island if it wasn't for this homestead that I'm living in. See, it's my grandparents's. It was a given, piece of property given to my grandmother by her uncle. And I promised them that as long as I am able to keep up the taxes, I would keep up the land. And I feel to myself that it would be just a waste of money to make my life or live it somewhere else and, ah, just keep up the taxes on the land here. And I don't like city life. I don't find any other places that I like better than here. It's quiet, peaceful.

And maybe I have green thumbs, because I like to be digging in the earth and planting something. And I like to be bothered with chickens. I bother with pigs, too. But I decide, after butchering the last one about a couple of months ago, I decide I wouldn't bother with that no more, because I'm getting older, a little bit lazier, and clumsier, so. I still keep my chickens.

I had two men to butcher it for me. I have it now what we call in pickle for a while. I have it in the salt pickle for a while, then I will take it out and smoke it. Those are the things that my grandfather used to do. He was a farmer, and he raised most of his foodstuffs. And I just like that kind of life, and that's why I bother around.

Now, I getta kick outta my chickens and gathering my eggs. My mother thinks I shouldn't bother with those kind of things, but since I retire and I don't have any children, I only have myself to care for. She thinks that I shouldn't bother with those things, but I think I'd jus drop if I didn't have something to keep me goin or keep me movin. And she's against me now workin the kind of work that I'm workin, but to have been with children so long when I was schoolteacher—I just have to have something to do. If it wasn't with children, I have to be around people. And that's why I went and took the course in training for family health worker. Um. I might not have bothered with it either, but I saw where Daufuskie needed it, and nobody else really accepted. So I thought there again I would try it out, and maybe I could convince or influence some of em younger to take the job. That I was fortunate with, because beginning the first of the month, I will be having a family health worker here on the island to assist me. And she is a young woman that I've taught.

And they're planning on getting a small boat, so we can have at least a nurse come to the island at least two or three times a week. Then the doctor wouldn't have to come but maybe once a month. But as it is now, doctor comes in every two weeks. Tomorrow is his day here.

Since Miss Grant went—she's a retired midwife—then the expecting mothers always taken away from the island at least a month before their time of birth. Yeah, it was quite a job with her, Miss Grant, because she also sells caskets. So I tell her she brings em into the world and she sends em out of the world.

We still have the old Jewish method: if you die today you're buried tomorrow. It's no embalming here on the island, unless you hire someone to come to the island. Now, as it is now, most of the people that die away from the island, they're not able to be brought back to the island. It might be very vicious, but they must be buried in Savannah or wherever they are, because it's so expensive to bring a funeral from Savannah. The boat in which to bring the dead person, you can get it no less than three hundred dollars.

They want to see a ferry to run daily, and that would bring more people to the island and maybe more business to the island. I love Daufuskie, and I would like to see it grow as other communities grow. That's my hope.

Years back they were oyster factories here on Daufuskie. And that's where most of the residents made their living—out of the river—oysters and shrimps, crabs and fish. We have Savannah River on our west and south; we have Calleybogey Sound on our north; and on our east we have Atlantic Ocean. I purchase my oysters from oyster factory in Bluston, South Carolina. It's not polluted there, neither at Hilton Head. Sometimes when I'm at Hilton Head, I'll purchase some there, from the factories there.

See, Savannah main channel runs out from Savannah by square of the Atlantic Ocean. Then when the tide flows out, the tide ebbs out, goes out to sea, well, it carries all the pollution from Savannah down. Then when it gets to what we call the bar—and that means where the tide turns, it begins flowing again—it flows back, and you still going straight up the Savannah River, it comes into Daufuskie Creek, and that's where Daufuskie oysters are polluted. They say that in nineteen seventy-three Daufuskie oysters'll be okay, because they are fighting the pollution, you know, in Savannah, with these industries like the paper mills and the cement plant, that turn out these oyster pollutions and chemicals into the water.

So now I buy my oysters off the island here. Make an oyster stew. Say, if you have a pint of oysters, you may fry about three or four strips of bacon or white salt meat, pork. Maybe pour off the drippings of fat to about a tablespoonful. Put in about a teaspoonful of flour, and you stir frequently so it won't burn and get to medium-brown. You then chop a medium-size onion and put into this flour with the bacon grease and let it cook for about five minutes. Then you wash your oysters and drain them. Add no water to the oysters. After you drain your oysters, you put your oysters into this sauce and add the seasoning: black pepper and maybe a taste of salt, and just cover it over a low heat and let it simmer, because the oysters have quite a bit of water in it. You let it simmer and cook slowly until all this water come out. Then you have a good oyster stew. But if you add water to it, these oysters will just draw up and become so skimpy that you won't have nothin but just a lot of liquid.

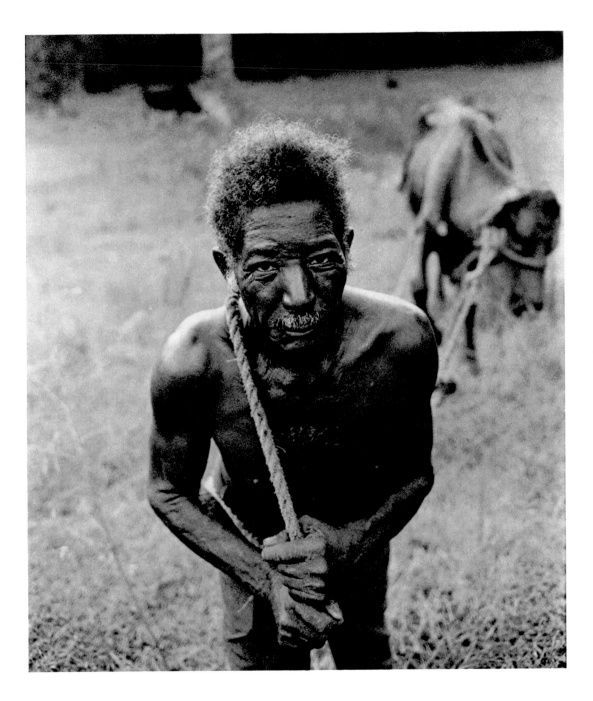

Indian Island, Maine

It is single file on the narrow bridge leading to Indian Island, and as I waited in my car for the approaching automobile to cross from the other side, I thought how beautiful a place it was, with dusk falling and the river shining and churning and there on the other side an island full of trees. I had been warned by a waitress in a restaurant that it was dangerous to go there. Her exact expression was something out of *High Noon:* "You know it's off limits to whites after sundown," she said, "and don't think I'm prejudiced. My best friend is an Indian, and she wouldn't go there."

It is still cowboys and Indians for many of the people on the mainland, and yet Indian Island seems on the surface like any other area of rural poverty. Three fat Indian ladies sit in front of the laundromat as I drive by, their hair dark and curly in home permanent waves, their lips red and bowed in acknowledgement of the fashion that *Glamour* says is sweeping the country. The only traces of Indian culture seem to be the tourist wares displayed at several roadside stands.

That is how it *seems;* how it *is* is different, and I could only discover part of that, for Indian culture is very elusive.

There is a tradition, when the Indians bury their dead, that there are no markers save the color of the earth, a deepish-red ochre clay that marks the grave site, the place where the spirit returns to the ground with the body and sanctifies it. Their culture is not treasured in book-lined libraries, in museums or concert halls or sculpture gardens. The sum of a man and his time lies buried with his body, a living presence in the earth.

Indian life and imagination are profoundly bound up with concepts and feelings about land and earth, not only in the religious sense of worship of spirits past and present, but in the cultural sense of habits performed during a life—the habits of hunting and fishing—habits of a life dependent on rivers, streams, and woodland. It is there the Indians of today are caught in a very special predicament unshared by any other group.

"To hunt and fish and be a man," a fifty-year-old Penobscot Indian told me, a man who works at odd jobs on the mainland, "that's all I want." He sits down wearily at the kitchen table in his house, a very old wooden structure badly in need of repair. Around him are piled Indian beading looms; boxes of instant mashed potatoes; very old, and seemingly broken appliances, washing machines, toasters; and some xeroxed copies of Indian treaties that look like tourist literature.

"You want to talk to an Indian? Don't talk to me. I'm no Indian. I *dream* of being an Indian. You call this Indian? Living like this?" His arm sweeps wide around his house, inviting a judgement. Then he opens a can of beer and turns on the television set. If the ghosts of childhood seem anachronistic to the average American, how much more so to an Indian? I wonder at his watching American westerns about redskins keemo-sabeeing in the white man's style, or leaning back to watch a baseball game of the "Braves" against the "Indians." The names seem all that is left of his culture.

"White makes right," he says, "that's all I ever heard."

"I thought that's what they told to Blacks," I said.

"Yeah," he smiles, "they told that to everybody." Then he tells me how he really has not the faintest notion of what Indian culture is supposed to be. He has the instincts, he says, but none of the values. I question this, and he shrugs again, "I want to hunt and fish and be a man. Just doing that means something."

His job in a factory on the mainland means nothing but some income, so he pursues it. He seems himself in a no man's land, without a culture, without a future, and without a past.

"Talk to the young people," he says, "They know things."

The young Indians today are noticeably vociferous about discovering their past and preserving it. At this strange time in history they are culturally fashionable among their white peers. Headbands and a yearning to return to the land abound. But these young Indian people must visit other reservations to find out what the culture was they lost; it has been that delicately preserved. They go to learn the lore and knowledge of how to survive in the out-of-doors, to gather the dying languages, the tales, the thoughts and attitudes, but most of all the techniques for physical survival from the old men before they die. It is only the oldest of the old men who know, and they are often reluctant to tell. There is a sense of privilege, a priestly guardianship about much of the knowledge they have. It is all the old men have.

I spent an afternoon looking for the sage of one tribe, a man nearing seventy-five, who among other things could cure almost any disorder from herbs gathered in the woods. I found him living in a tarpaper shack. He was drunk; it was a weekend he was not eager to see me, but he was cordial. He waved an eagle feather in my face and told me it has been awarded him as a great honor. He repeated this three times, and when I tried to find out what it was for, he said only that it was for what he *knew*. He was suspicious of me, of course, and did not wish to reveal any of its meaning.

Beneath his dirty clothes, his tobacco-stained face, the slack gaze of someone drunk, was a faded intensity that belonged to a pride now gone. I had gone looking for him, expecting to find a sage of heroic stature, bursting with dignity and superior bone structure, a perfect replica of the Indian as tragic hero. But tragedy is too grand an expectation; it puts too fine a cast on the legacy of American history. The evidence of that grave act, the theft of a society's knowledge of itself, its meaning, here seemed disproportional to the act itself. One still expects some kind of heroism in its victims, some noble line. But you cannot deny a man his life work and culture and expect to find dignity. I did not find a noble Indian. I found a drunken old man, living in a cluttered shack, who carved statues out of stone for the Catholic Church.

Sometimes when I think of him, standing there, shrunken in a wool plaid shirt, hanging onto the eagle feather as though trying to remind himself of the authority it once held, I think that in part, perhaps, it was his last defense against the theft that he would not let me see more.

That old man was at a strange point in history, at a point when he sensed his own people's resurging interest in their culture, at a time when there were few left who knew what it was.

However frail and remotely known, that culture nevertheless proved to be the major force in the life of a young woman, Eugenia Thompson, who had grown up on Indian Island, the land of the Penobscot Nation, and who recently at the age of thirty left the mainland and her middle-class life to search for the vestiges of that culture.

The move came as a surprise. She had graduated from the University of Maine with a B.A. in psychology, had married a white lawyer, had lived with him in their comfortable house, borne three children and seemed ready to accept the standards of white, middle-class American life. She is an Indian, and of course, he knew that; knew too, that she had been born and raised on Indian Island. But why all of a sudden the need to return to the land of the Penobscot Nation? And not only to move to Indian Island, but to ask her husband to give up his law practice.

Eugenia Thompson had concluded she could find no cultural meaning for herself and her family in the typical, middle-class American life style. She had felt in her life as an Indian child, even in a vanishing culture, more contact with what she experienced as the fundamental forces in life than she could ever hope to find in the life she and her husband then lived. She saw people in towns and cities hopelessly dependent on others for food, services, housing—all the necessities of life—and totally ignorant of techniques for self-sufficiency. Eugenia Thompson says she does not miss the conveniences of modern life, since to her they are only cumbersome. She says she is trying in every way to learn to live off the natural resources around her, to learn the skills and techniques necessary to survive, and to rediscover a cultural identity.

The first part of this interview took place in August, two days after she returned from the hospital with her fourth child. We sat in a camper, which served as the bedroom for the children and her mother-in-law. It was alongside the trailer where she and her husband sleep and where he has a room for his very limited law practice. When she decided to resume the Indian life on the island, she decided Ken could join her only if he gave up a practice based on white man's law, a law that had in her opinion violated Indian property rights. Now Ken Thompson does mostly Indian things, and they try to survive on sixty dollars a week.

The second part of the interview took place in October, when they had moved into the house next door for the winter. Ken and Eugenia sat in the kitchen, while the children ran in and out, curious, torn between the television and the visitors. It struck me that Eugenia Thompson was one of the freest women I had ever met. Free in the sense of a willingness to talk about all aspects of her life with a strong sense of conviction and no sense of defense. The most extraordinary thing perhaps was the absence of any self-consciousness. She felt no inhibitions about discussing everything in front of her children.

The house was not neat; indeed it seemed not to have any sense of order to me; yet there were no signs of confusion or distress among its inhabitants, so I must assume there was an order not immediately clear to me. She does her housework when she gets to it; she moves on a priority of feelings, which may be an old Indian way, but it is also a new, this-generation American way. The household was what an open household should be—warm and loving, with a mother committed to growth and renewal in a refreshingly unobtrusive way.

Eugenia and Ken Thompson

EUGENIA: **M**y mother left us when I was two years old. I was just a baby and my brother was five. My aunt and grandmother took care of us. My father did, too, but he died when he was forty-four, had heart trouble. So we grew up with the family here on the island, you know, here, sort of taking care of each other.

And then when I was thirteen, we moved to Gardiner, so my aunt could get a job. I went to high school and on to college. Worked five years as a social worker. My husband worked in the Department of Indian Affairs, and then later as a lawyer.

From nineteen sixty-nine to nineteen seventy I was a Ford Fellow under the Ford Leadership Program. And I started that in September of sixty-nine, traveling all over the country, finding out why Indian kids dropped out of high school at a higher rate than white children. There are many, many reasons: economic reasons, social reasons, psychological reasons. You know, you can take any child and give a reason for it. But the underlying reason—if I could tie these all together—was the identity of the child, that the Indian child had.

The child is Indian, comes from an Indian background. So when he does enter school, he goes into a foreign existence, that has no correlation to himself, to what his background was, possibly is, and possibly could be in the future. Also, the mothers worked, so they were never at home, and this has caused a breakup in the structure of the family, in the historical structure of the Indians. And it caused a breakdown in the languages and a breakdown in the passing on of the history and traditions. When you get mothers and fathers away from the homes, working in far-distant parts of the country, you don't have any continuity in your land and in your history.

My mother left because she had to survive, because her social structure had broken down, and there was nothing to look forward to, to carry on, no reason to survive. Survival for the Indian was easier when the structure as a whole was closer knit, because they all looked out for each other. They were able to hunt and trap and share with each other. Now it's broken down even further. Except, we do share some emotions.

I like living here. It's my home. And even with the population, the people cross the bridge, you know, getting closer and closer, to me it's a pretty safe place.

It's like the last stronghold, the last fort that we have to really take care of. Because if we let our guards down, they'll come marching up and take the rest of our lands, our gardens, and we'll have no more room.

We don't have to live off nature because of the availability of jobs here, you know. They want every Indian man doing a project. They want to do studies, you know. They want him to work. That seems to be the in thing this year: grab an Indian and let's work him.

Reminds me of a story about the Indian that was out on the lake fishing. And this man went and caught up and said, "What are you doing out there?"

Indian said, "I am fishing."

So he said, "You shouldn't be out there fishing. You should be out working in the factory."

So the Indian said, "What would I be doing?"

The other man said, "Well, I could train you to work in the factory."

And the Indian said, "Then what?"

"Well, you could save up your money and buy a house, a TV, car, all those things."

The Indian said, "Then what?"

"Well, you could get into your car and drive."

"Then what?"

"Then," the man said, "you could go into retirement."

"Retire? And then what?"

"Well, then you could go fishing, hunting."

Well, the Indian is doing that already.

This will be my second year in nature school, so to speak. A second grader. And I don't know very much, but I know a little bit. And I am very proud of that little bit that I do know—just learning where the berries are out and what to do with them and how you could store them, how you can prepare them after you're finished, you know.

There's an old man, Senabe. He's the same age as my father. And he knows a lot of the herbs, a lot of the medicines. When I had poison ivy, I had it all over

my arms, my legs, and my face and most of my back, and I really rubbed it all over. I had it real good. I had all sorts of stuff—I got things from the drug store—and it runs its course in ten days. But on the third day he said, "You should have told me you were in such misery. You should have told me you had poison ivy."

And I said, "I couldn't get out of the door."

So he said, "You should have sent word down."

So he went out in the woods, and he brought some medicine back and steeped it for me. And he had me put it on my places there. And it coated my skin all brown.

But he said, "This will help it, relieve the itching and dry it up."

And sure enough it did. Practically overnight. And I got on my feet again. That's one of the medicines. Right on the front doorstep. And there are the other medicines, too, that a person could use. I could go and pick it up, pick it off the trees here. I just haven't had the time. But you know, there's no need of money to buy these medicines. You can use your two legs and go get some.

It's a matter of choice that I made. For an Indian, for a real Indian, if you are going to be a way, be a way. You can't be both. If you're both, you have a confusing identity. Like when I left the reservation, always, there was always the nagging: what was going on back here in this little community here? What were the people thinking? How were they doing back here? What is it to be an Indian? You should be proud you're an Indian. So sure, I knew I was an Indian, but it wasn't anything to be proud of. How could I be proud of all these treaties that were broken?

The very fact that Ken was willing to move back with me enabled me to work out these things. It would be a little harder if I had to do it alone. But he said he did want to come. And in a way it's been harder for him because he's had to give up quite a bit of his material things. We had two cars, Volkswagen bus, and eight-room house, color TV, dishwasher, you know, the whole, the whole—you know.

Well, this is a camper, and it sleeps six people. His mother sleeps there, and the children all sleep there, and we put down a couple of mattresses. The front part here is Ken's law office, and the other part is where we have all of our clothes and closets and the bathroom on the end of it, hooked into a septic tank.

We have a septic tank, but no running water. We run after it. We have a hose coming over from Martin's house. And in the wintertime, we'll have to run after it in buckets or something. But if we did have running water, that would be another bill we would have to pay. Having our own septic tank, too, and not tying into the sewerage in Oldtown is also one less bill we have to pay.

We don't have any electricity. And our gas ran out a couple of weeks ago, so we cook over the open fire. That's because we don't have the money to get the gas. We would rather spend the money on building that one-room house for this winter up on the hill, up on the ledge there.

Last winter we took our income-tax money and put it as a down payment for a trailer. So we were able to live in it for about three months rent free, till they came and took it. They took it in July, end of June. From then on we lived here.

My husband works just part time now. He doesn't take any court cases. He just helps people with bankruptcies and wage-earning cases. And he's helpful in several businesses. He gets about sixty dollars a week.

And we eat out of the garden. And come this winter, we'll probably be eating some rabbits, chickens, eggs here. And the men have been good about bringing muskrat around, fish. And probably soon someone will have some deer. Deer meat. Moose meat, beaver—all sorts of meat. Men go hunting. This year Ken could go hunting, too. We have a gun. And if I get up and around, I think I'll probably go, too. But we have rabbits right here that we breed. Chickens. And our garden. And I've canned little heads, about twelve quarts of little heads, lettuce and cabbage. And I made some watermelon-rind relish. And canned peas. Plan to can some more out of the garden here. Put up some berries. And when the apples come up, we'll probably put up some apple jelly or dried apples. Dried squash.

The dried milk is given to us. And over at Martin's house, there's a room up there, and half of it's filled with dried milk and dried corn, corn meal, flour, beans, all sorts of beans, about five varieties of beans. That's from the federal government. People don't use it. They don't need to use it because they have income. But the federal government gives it to us. This is the treaty, treaty items. They come by and say, "Do you want this?" So we take it, and we store it up there. And comes winter, we'll probably be baking a lot of beans. Soup and stuff. We've got this canned pork and canned beef. Comes all prepared, all cooked. All you have to do is open it up and cook it.

Surplus food is what it is. And anybody here who wants it can get it. The men especially can get it, depending on their income. If you have a certain amount

98.

of income, you're entitled to it. The women who are married to white people cannot get it here—not entitled to any surplus food. The federal doesn't recognize the woman, Indian woman. It's immoral, really. This is the decision a woman makes when she married underneath the State of Maine law. And women don't realize that.

Neither do they realize, the young Indians realize, that at the age of eighteen they do not have to register to vote or register to be drafted. They go into town to do it, and their fathers probably did it, too. But they don't have to do it, you know. But they do it out of habit. Not because they're pressured into it or because it's a law for them, but just because out of habit they do it. And that's the shame of it all. They don't realize those things. So when I tell them these things, they think I'm rabble-rousing. But it's true. And they all go around and get drafted or get married.

Which I did. I got married. I didn't realize at the time—if I were getting married tomorrow, under the same conditions, I think I would want to be married by one of the chiefs here and not by the State of Maine law. At that time I didn't realize it. I was in a different country anyway.

Here is a different country from the rest of Maine, once you step off from the island here, the Penobscot Nation. We have a system of government here, which is recognized by the State of Maine. It was set up by the State of Maine and was paid for by the State of Maine. But I don't recognize it. We have our own government. It's all written down, and people just haven't had a need to use it just yet. We have chiefs and war chiefs and sub chiefs and clan heads, clan members. They're all here. But there is no need to use it. The people don't see any need to get together and use these things. They're too busy watching TV, going to the movies. Great answers, you know.

But when the time comes, it'll be there. People that do know these things, we'll be ready. The younger people are working more for it now. They're working to preserve these things. A few of them knew we've got to get together. Young people want to do something to get our nation going again, you know, get so we know who our chiefs are.

Traditions are being made today. Legends are still being made. Like there's an old Indian woman up there that still delivers babies, a midwife more or less. And she has powers that way and can cast spells and things like this. She's still holding on, you know. We still talk about her. In that condition, we still see her. And so, we make her into this, you know, make her be a legend. And the kids, they hear us talking about it, and they knew because they had seen her and knew her powers, what she was doing. She can cast spells and take spells off. She can heal, you know. She can heal sores. And I

don't know what kind of other things she can do. But she knows all the medicines out in the woods. She's always going out hunting some. And she can make it hard for you, yeah. Make it hard for you.

There is this kind of power among Indian people. That's my belief. Because our people have been here for so many years, and our spirits are so numerous now, it's impossible to count them. Maybe the spirits are still in the trees, still in the ground, in the animals. Look around. There's another world we don't see, we don't hear, we don't know about. I have been hearing from many Indian medicine people, you know, that there is this world of existence. There's a world of our ancestors, world of departed people. They still exist. Really die, pass away, go on to a heaven or a hell. So all these ancestral spirits are still here.

The spirits are here. That's why an Indian has to come back to his own land. There's a man teaches high school to Indian kids in Bangor. He says every three or four weeks they get restless and they have to come home. So they come home, step forward on their ground, get their strength back, you know. Then they go back, go to high school in Bangor. Be all right for a little while longer. All right. So he says, "I think there is something to do with that land," you know. "The spirits are there." And I really believe that, too.

There was a dream a little boy had here. And it was a period of time where there was a lot of activity going on among Indian people all over the country. This little boy dreamt that down by the cemetery he saw all these hands coming up out of the ground all over the place. All these hands. So it was interpreted all the ancestors wanted to help. People. They wanted to help. So he wasn't scared after that. It's no good to be scared.

What I'm trying to do now, what I've been trying to do since nineteen sixty-nine, is to request the State of Maine to furnish me with the treaty items. In eighteen twenty, when Maine became a state, they said, "Well, we'll give you these items every October; as long as you remain a nation, you can have them."

The month of October, this month here, we're supposed to be getting, you know, five hundred bushels of corn, fifteen barrels of wheat flour, seven barrels of clear pork, one hogshead of molasses, and one hundred yards of double broadcloth to be a red color one year, blue the next, and so on. Alternately, fifty good blankets (I hope they don't have smallpox in em—they're supposed to be good blankets), one hundred pounds of gunpowder, four hundred pounds of shot, sixty boxes of chocolate, one hundred and forty pounds of tobacco, and fifty dollars in silver. That's supposed to be coming each year. So I say that we shouldn't even be asking for welfare. I should be getting these things every October.

We used to be owning six miles each side of the river. Also, according to the treaty made by the State of Maine with the Penobscots, that was supposed to be held for us, you know, for ever and ever, you know, as long as we remain a nation. We're still a nation, and they still haven't kept up their bargain.

If we all pushed together on this particular issue, you know, and did indeed become leaseholders, holding the lands along the river, which are settled by white people, we could indeed become quite wealthy.

KEN: In Maine the feeling is that this land didn't belong to the Indians, that the Indians were just using it. And that when the English came over and the French, that just by drawing up deeds, this changed everything. The deeds determined who actually owned something.

They figured if the Indians had owned the land, they would have some kind of a deed and recording system. But that's foolish. I mean, it's just a matter of interpretation, you know, or opinion—really who has a stronger army to defend, you know, which way you do it.

And the Indians are noted for selling the same piece of land the same day even to two or three different people. And the reason was, they thought it was foolish, and they thought they were getting the best deal, because they thought anybody can use the land.

EUGENIA: You see, the Indians was lettin em use it for however they wanted to use it—to go ahead and use it, you know, if they wanted to catch a fish, to go ahead and use it. But then white men, they wanted it forever, you know. They didn't want to share it with anybody else. Wanted it all to themselves.

All we have left now is our identity and our land. We have our traditional dress, but this is being copied, you know, by department stores having fringed coats and headbands, moccasins, the whole works. And we've lost our language, because of the education in our schools. The children nowadays aren't being taught the Indian language in the homes. So they learn English, you know, a foreign language. And this is all they grow up with, so they therefore don't retain any of their Indian native language. Then the customs and traditions are slowly going, replaced by white man's cultures and traditions.

The last thing that the Indian tribe or the Indian nation has left is their land, the thing that they identify with, the thing they go back to when times are tough in the cities. When a death occurs in the family, they'll always go back home, you know, and take their relative's body back for burial in the ancient cemetery.

KEN: The Penobscots used to cremate their people. And then they'd have this red ochre, they called it. It was like a red rock. And they'd mix the ashes with this and bury it. And sometimes they'd put things with it, you know, things that the person might need or the spirit might need, you know.

And they're very careful about digging up here. For instance, they've had places where they've dug and there've been red streaks in the ground. And of course this is from this red ochre. And people get very upset about that, when people start digging around, you know, turning up this thing.

EUGENIA: It's back to earth, you know, back to nature, return to nature of things that are supposed to be there.

Here on this island there's nobody telling you what to do with your freedoms, really. If you want to wear your sweatshirt seven days, well, wear your sweatshirt for seven days and wear it again. Turn it inside out. It's a freedom from people imposing their views, their sets of values upon you.

We don't have any set of rigid rules, any legal court system or any educational system. It helps to educate the children, yet on the other extreme, it takes away their freedom, so to speak. And the educational system, which we have down on the island here in the school, which has twenty-five children in it, takes away from the freedom of the child to have his own experience. He has to share it, you know, with all these other little children. There's only one teacher.

In a big city there's so many regulations that you live under, because there are so many people there. And they're very oppressed, depressed—a very depressed area to live in. And you feel it. There is oppression here, too, because people are allowing this oppression to happen. There is poverty, if you want to call it poverty. The reason why they call it living in poverty is that it's somebody else's values being imposed upon us. And if this is the only value you can see, living the way we do is poverty—having no income is poverty in your value.

But our value is different. Our highest value is not the highest income you can obtain. This is not our value at all. I tell you it's a value of freedom, you know—to allow my husband freedom from the oppression of working eight hours a day under a set schedule for an institution that possibly does not grant him the freedom or license to speak freely for himself or for other people, but has a set regulation that he has to speak. This is oppression. And what we've found here is more or less freedom from this type of a life.

Because I am a Penobscot Indian, my loyalty lies with my land, whereas Ken's never had any loyalties coming out of this land, you know, never had any relationship with it. So he feels different than I do. So I feel very strongly about things like federal intervention here or federal programs coming here, because I can see this as minor steps, however minor they are, but steps toward the federal government regulating our affairs.

KEN: I tend to be very realistic on things. I know we have to eat, for instance; and you know, sometimes that takes money. Like I hate to see the federal government get too involved in the state, but here, if there're people out of work and there's a program available and they want me to help em get it, financially, I'll help them get it. I may not like to see the program come in, but I feel, you know, that these people have as much right to live and to get the kind of life they want. And, you see, these people here don't always agree with Gene. Many do and many do to some degree. But the thing is that some people want something else. And I think I can accept them pretty well. If that's what they want, I don't try to impose my feelings either way.

EUGENIA: Things have different value to the Indian. Like the turtle is important to the Indian. I don't know why exactly. Of course, it lives very close to the earth. Matter of fact, it hibernates inside the earth and lives forever, you know—I mean, not forever, but we've got turtles down in the pond here lived for a hundred years. Big turtles, you know, right down here in the pond. They live here in the pond that to some of the kids around here is nothing but a cesspool. But they don't understand the workings of nature. To the turtle it's just part of the earth, and they can live on it. It's provided for them. And they go their own way, you know. They don't come in our house for a cup of coffee, you know, or impose their turtle ways on us. But they live according to their own way.

KEN: The water is polluted in a sense, from houses, you know, from flushes and things like that and sewerage, but not in the sense of DDT and stuff like that.

EUGENIA: Just oversaturated with Indians. But, you know, the turtle is a scavenger. Cleaning up the land is his duty, what he's supposed to do. It's his responsibility for that part of the land. Same way the Indians have a certain responsibility. Like I feel a responsibility to this land here.

We all have to live here. The birds have to live here and the dogs, you know, and the bobcats and the fish, even the turtles, you know, all live here in this community. And I relate to them because I need them. I need the turtles to clean up my pond for me. I need the birds to get the insects. And I need the trees. And this is all part of my identity. It may be very much a physical identity, but to me it's also a spiritual identity, cause all these living things have a spirit in them. They're all living things. Even the trees are living.

A little child will know these things, you know, standing by the road, listening to the trees. Sometimes they'll dance when the wind moves a tree, they'll dance.

I was brought up to believe that spiritual ways were going to church every Sunday. But now I realize you can't really learn spiritual values only inside a church. You have to get right out there where the spirits are. To me the spirits are living things, you know. The spirits are trees. The spirits aren't wooden crosses with people hanging from them, blood and everything. Or priests in Rome talking about whether to do it or not.

I'm not a member of any women's liberation movement or anything like that. But to me, you know, primarily being an Indian woman, I have certain responsibilities to my children. And women's liberation, I think—you know, I've heard a lot about it and read a lot about it, and to me these are women who are trying to break into a man's world more or less, who are trying to get into a system that has oppressed men by having them work so many hours a day, you know. I think the men are the ones that should be freed.

Freedom in sexuality is more noticeable here on this particular reservation or among Indians in general, I suppose. I've noticed it. And I think Ken has noticed it. There's no inhibitions here.

I think growing up here on this particular reservation gave me a great deal of freedom sexually. This is the primary identity the child sees in his parents. And also he observes other children growing up. And it's only later when philosophy identity changes, you know, or grows, one is able to express it, you know.

The primary expression of children growing up is the sexual expression. It's very much part of life, you know, in order for life to go on, you know. This is a very basic drive that children have, that men and women have, the birds have, you know, and other animals. And it's only when the missionaries go over and said, "You better do it this way," you know, men on top and women on bottom, you know.

KEN: Margaret Mead, for instance, has mentioned that there's what they call a missionary way, and that's a term picked up by similar groups that she's visited. And apparently people never gave it a second thought how you were supposed to do this, you know. But it's just that once the missionaries came, it got this particular name, cause anything else was either sinful or had connotations of sinful.

EUGENIA: But to me the ideal is to be able to find sexual pleasure in life in general, sex meaning an attraction a person has for his own sex or an opposite sex, I think, at each age and any time.

Now maybe at the age of eighty, you know, I'll still have cravings for somebody else who is eighty. Now, who knows? But this is the freedom that we have here, that allows us to express ourselves freely, you know. Like talking about picketing, which in your terms might be a fart. But here even the kids talk about going to urinate, you know. And they do it in a group of adults. And there is no reservations or inhibitions about it, cause it's a natural way. No body shame.

Sacramento, California

On a tree-lined street in Sacramento, in the hot, bright California sun, I see the place. It is a small, red-roofed house, with a two-story second house behind it. There are tricycles in the yard, and a dog runs out when the car pulls into the drive. It looks like a typical middle-class home. I ask for Charlie Fitzgerald.

He is waiting for me in the small living room of his three-room apartment on the second floor of the rear building. He is a white haired, impeccable man in a bright blue tie with large white polka dots and suspenders. His blue eyes sparkle when we are introduced, and when I tell him he is dapper, he smiles and tells me, "Makes you feel like a new man having clothes." He turns around so I can get a full view and then he says, "And I'm in terrific shape," as he reaches over to touch the floor with his hands. "I'm eighty-six," he says, this spry, alert person who looks no more than sixty. He has spent fifty-eight years in prison.

First sentenced to thirteen years for allegedly shooting a deputy in Montana, he was out of prison for a few years when he was sent to Folsom (California State Prison at Folsom) for reportedly shooting a police officer who had climbed the running board of a car in which Charlie and three other men were sitting and had ordered them to the police station. The charge was bootlegging liquor. The other two men in the car "fingered" Charlie, and he got a life sentence.

He was finally paroled last August. "If the charge had been shooting a regular citizen," Charlie says to me, "I would've been out long ago." Then he looks off into space.

"What did you think about most of the time?" I ask.

"Getting out."

"How could you endure the endless denials of parole, the waiting?"

"Only do one day at a time, that's how, and never trust any of the inmates." His mistrust is based on the simple observation that when men are desperate they'll do anything. Charlie Fitzgerald now lives in a halfway house for convicts, bridging the time in which they return from prison to the world, or at least to another world. He is blunt about wanting to get out of the house into some other kind of living arrangement, because as he puts it, "I want to get away from the kind of men I've spent my life with."

He is angry about the notoriety his long prison term has brought him and refuses to tell me the name of his home town, "because, who knows, I might want to go back some day."

When the press and radio and TV reporters rushed him at the gates upon his release from Folsom, he was not happy. Except for one surprise. His eyes light up when he tells me that a lady saw him on television and was immediately smitten. She sent him her telephone number and address, and he says to me, "Who knows, I'll probably look her up. I'd like to get married some day."

Although he is eighty-six, he seems to have no fear of life or time running out. It seems to him rather that his life has been stalled, like a good car on too steep a hill, and now that it is running again, he has every intention of continuing the original journey. Ten minutes or sixty-one years, he clearly cannot think of time in any conventional way. If he had, one thinks, surely he could not have survived so well. He is not defeated and told me he was never depressed the entire time he was in prison. It seems to me he began to think of it as a kind of cold storage, for he is like nothing so much as Sleeping Beauty awakening to the world after a long sleep; only the world is different.

When I ask him if he thinks he has changed much in the course of his imprisonment he says he thinks he's about the same as when he went in. In this case, defying change seems to be a way of keeping a grasp on life itself, maintaining a kind of interior integrity, if only by a stubborn refusal to acknowledge the system had any effect at all.

The little pleasures, like clothes, are great indeed. I am surprised, however, that the world is not a more bewildering place. When I suggest this, he says, "Well, I could see the planes, you know, from the yard. I looked up and saw the sky." He explains that is why he was not as surprised as everyone expected when his parole officer took him to the airport as the first place to visit upon his release. His parole officer is a man who clearly enjoys Charlie's company. Charlie's rediscovery of the changes, particularly technological, that have happened on the outside during his prison term reminds his parole officer that the world, as it is, has not always been so; it reminds him, too, in seemingly small ways, of the endurance of that quality in human life sometimes called the élan vital, sometimes called the vital spark, the resistance to despair, which usually has romantic labels because it finally *is* mysterious. When Charlie Fitzgerald first got into his parole officer's car, the car door light went on.

"What's that for?" he said.

"So you know the door is open."

"Hey, that's good, isn't it?" he says.

He is equally approving of elevator buttons.

Charles Fitzgerald

I done some thirteen years in Montana, then I done forty-five years and seven months in Folsom.

Montana, I was in fer killin this deputy sheriff. Had another guy with me. I turned him loose. Never sent me a nickel, never heard from him. Everybody in that place at that time carried a gun. Cow punchin town, shippin town. Gun brawl, deputy sheriff got killed. I rode the beef. Thirteen years.

Folsom, killed a police. I got forty-six years this time. I done thirty-eight years in one cell. I asked for my first job after twenty years in the brick yard, and the deputy warden wouldn't give it to me. He told the warden that I'd cut somebody's head off. I seen the warden, and I asked him, I says, "Who's this guy's head I'm gonna cut off?" I said, "I don't know I got me an enemy. Who is he?"

"Oh," he says, "forget about it."

So I forget about it after that. So I stayed in that cell for years after that. Cards all over that cell. My sister would send me cards every Christmas down in Los Angeles. Guy by the name of Rodrigas, he was sendin me cards regular. He was here, got out. And he had his sister send me cards when he got out.

When I first come, all they had was buckets in the cells. Used to have to carry em out every mornin an dump em. If you had a cell mate, you'd exchange—he'd carry em one day, you'd carry em the next. Then they done away with that. Now they got toilets in there an you got a wash basin: cold water. And you got a bed. An you fix it up the way you want it. Pictures. I had pictures all over my cell. Christmas cards. Half a foot from the ceiling all the way down to two feet from the floor, all the way around. Had calendars. They send em in, Church over there gives a Catholic calendar, desk calendar, everlastin calendar.

I've had one visit here since I been here—a Jehovah Witness. He come in here once to see me. Never did come back. He got my name outta the paper. He called on me. I got a visit. And I told him, I says, "You see that bull over there? Easy go for you: all you gotta do is stand up there and look wise, and if you see a guy taking a piece of bread," I said, "if you wanna be dirty enough you can write him up. Otherwise, you can pass him up an draw yourself nine hundred dollars a month, jus for standin around lookin wise." I said, "That's better than what you're doin. You ain't makin a

livin. Why don't you come here an take a job an get on the taxpayers' roll, get some of this gravy train here. Regular slave market. If you like to herd slaves, jus come right here."

I tried to escape in nineteen twenty-nine, an I got tipped off, an I dummied up ever since. I kept still, never associated with anybody, never tried it again. Spent my time alone. You could say it's solitary, my bein alone, but I had my exercise every day. Every day I'd go out in the yard. Oh, we stayed out there all day, six, seven hours.

Convicts are different: they don't stick. They go out, they don't stick, they don't help one another. The minute they leave the gate, they forget you. I had a lotta acquaintance, no friends. I'm goin on eighty-six years old, I haven't found a friend yet. People misquote this friendship business. A friend is a guy who'd sacrifice his life for you, if he's really a friend of yours. Then there's a fairweather friendship: it's how much you got in your pocket. If you're holdin well in your pocket, you can feed em, clothe em, help em out, they all be your friends. But friendship don't go no further than that. They misabuse the word. You don't pay em, they'll scandalize you. If you help em out, you're a sucker.

I got put in the hole after I tried to get out. I did about ninety days in the hole. I think we went four days on bread an water. Then they give you the feed. They start to feed you regular, but you make any noise in there, they put you back on bread'n water again.

It's dark in there. You got one bucket, one water bucket—you got two buckets: one is for the urine and so forth, an the other one is drinking water. So you gotta watch out you don't make any mistakes.

You can put a pin down on the floor and crawl around an try to find it or somethin, keep your mind occupied.

Today they baby em too much.

Nowadays, outside, well, it's jus like days a yore far as I'm concerned. It's faster an bunch of wild maniacs runnin around, no consideration for anybody else —the human race, the way they drive them cars. Nowadays they all wanna see what they can get outta your pocket.

No more horse. No more street cars. The street cars are better—you know when you're gonna get home. That bus—if it's crowded, it'll keep right on goin, won't stop. And the people don't walk.

I walk two to five miles a day, and take my exercise every Sunday

night. I don't overdo it. I take push-ups, kick-ups. Push-ups on each arm: two on this arm, two on that. Twist my neck. I can palm my hands on the floor bendin over.

I was never sick a day outside of the day I broke my back goin over the fence. Guy locked me into the alley and he locked the gate an I tried to get out. Instead of puttin my feet down, I slid down, like shoot-the-shoots, hit a three-inch pipe and threw my feet off an threw me back. Took my hands off an I went out in mid-air.

In there, you wanna keep up, keep readin, keep your mind active, be doin somethin. No struggle to me. I jus keep a readin. I never let anything bother me or worry me. Only thing worry me is gettin outta there.

They had work. I was on the rock pile, breakin stone, cuttin stone. They put me back on the derrick pushin the derrick around for years. Then I went upstairs in upper shop and worked in there, barber shop. Forty years up there. You could call it work if you want or you could call it jus fooling around. Jus a slave market. It's jus to keep you occupied, keep your mind workin.

A prison is no different than any other city. The prison is a city in itself. It's a confined city. You have a canteen, where you can go buy anything you want within the prison regulations. You have a library there, you have a public bathhouse there, you have a barber shop there, you have a shoe shop there, you have a clothin shop, a boiler room to furnish you hot water. You have a laundry there. It's a city within a city is what it is. An anything that could be got out here in the city can be got in prison: whiskey, narcotics, money, gamblin, anything.

What kept me alive is only one thing I can say: take care of your own business, not gettin involved in gamblin so you can't pay your bills. Then you won't have no trouble. You can make it. Stay by yourself, have a few pals, that's all. Don't mingle too much. Dog eat dog. Goodtime Charlie, you're payin all the bills.

I'm no different now. I don't think so. Think I'm the same man as when I went in. One thing is I'm a little older an I ain't playin the part of the samaritan. I'm a bird now. I fly by myself. Ever watch a bird? He takes care of himself. He don't feed the other ones. He's watchin out for himself. An you play the part of the samaritan, you feed em, they call you sucker or chump. They take the kindness for weakness.

It feels real good to be free. I wanna see what's goin on in the world.

I can go out an see the animals—I can go out an see the zoo, take a look at the animals, the original animals for once, see what they're doin, take in the sights, an look around.

They took me over to one of these cottages over here. Gonna rent one of em, Senior Citizens. It's a nice place. But I'd be better off gettin one furnished. Have to furnish it. Live the rest of my life in peace. Hurray for me.

Montpelier, Vermont

The large, old farmhouse is on the top of a hill in the beautiful valleys of Vermont. It is ideal country, green and unspoiled, and the hill people, as the townspeople of Montpelier call them, are known for a certain stubborn independence. There may be a streak of that, his mother says, in Steve, her nineteen-year-old son, who dropped out of college because he wasn't learning enough. Instead, he decided to continue his education in his own way. He works at whatever he can find. He is building a roof when I meet him. And he hitchhikes.

He approaches hitchhiking somewhat as one would a profession. On the wall of this farmhouse is an enormous map, full of red and blue marks indicating routes and turnpike exits and entrances. It shows how many miles he has covered and where he plans to go. It also contains notations of where the best exits and entrances are for rides, on what roads, at what intersections, and in what towns the cops are tough, where they'll lock you up, and where they'll leave you alone. This is the master map. He also carries many maps with him. Like many people in America today, he has learned to live on very little money: hitchhiking and crashpadding with friends, usually in college towns, is one way to do it.

Who does and doesn't pick up a hitchhiker, whether they have sons or daughters that age or not, in what Howard Johnson's, in what states, what they say and what they don't say in the special intimacy a car can produce reveals much about the changing social rhythms of American life. For the moment, hitchhiking has replaced college as his source of education. It is a curious education, which is usually the best kind.

Steve Edwards

I hitchhike. To get from one place to another. You get to see what people think, what people do. You find out things that you wouldn't find out normally. You learn about things like truck hijacking. And you meet people that you wouldn't meet otherwise at all. It's cheap. It's fascinating. It's sometimes dangerous, but not very often.

Now, I'll tell you, I've gotten rides with some very nice-looking young ladies. I'll tell you that. Yes. Now, as far as what was in their minds, you know,

I'm not positive. Now, I generally will try at talking to them on probably what is the unsex side of what they could be thinking. In other words, I would not be too hasty to take something as a sexual overture. Well, I don't blindly ignore it—it takes some effort. There haven't been hundreds who make these overtures, but yes, there have been some.

Men, too, a couple. There was one guy I was riding with, and he said—he was talking about all the kinds of things that he and the boys used to do in school and stuff. This guy was some sort of a salesman or something. One of the things he said to me, he said, "Been laid much?" This is when I was in high school, you know. And so then we were just discussing along, and then the guy sort of switched subjects a little bit. The guy says to me and at the same time reaches over his right hand, he says, "Must have a nice set, kid." Afterwards I thought about it. Wow! That was weird.

Self-preservation is part of this. You want to be able to learn as many ways as you can to relate to different kinds of people, so you survive longer, depending on the places you're in. You learn by trying and relating to people. I learned just the other day that telling people stories goes over really well, if they're at least, you know, halfway true. And there are a lot of people who sort of like a story, but they don't want a big yarn or something. They do enjoy stories.

Then the people that you ask for rides, like in Howard Johnson places, they have a really hard time saying no. So most of the time they lie to you. There's the ones that my friend DC calls the no-roomer-rappers. And those are the people that say, "Sorry, no room," and then you see them drive by, and they go right out front in their station wagons with just them. Station wagon. Nothing else.

Then there's the company-car people. You know, "Sorry, company car." And then they go out—they go driving by. "Company car" because the insurance—you wouldn't be covered if you were riding in this car and all this business, which is probably in a lot of cases true, but there's a lot of other people that, I think, use it as an excuse.

I've been arrested only three times, but I've come close to it a number of others. You get the old five-minute-warning routine in a lot of places. And the five-minute warning is murder. And they love to bring them in. This is where a policeman, or two policemen better yet, they come up to you and they say, "Are you

hitchhiking?" And after that they'd say, "If you're out here in five minutes, you're in trouble." And that's all they say to you.

You're supposed to evaporate. It's such a great calculation, a calculated thing on their part, because they can go in and sit calmly and eat a hamburger, and then they can come out in five minutes, and you're sure to be there unless you ran off into the woods somewhere, which is what DC and I, when we went out to Ohio in May, we went out and went to sleep.

It was four o'clock in the morning, and the cop says, "Are you looking for rides?" or something like that.

We said, "Yes." And this is on the New York Thruway.

And then the guy said, "Well, when I come back out here, you'd better not be here." You know, that old routine. "Otherwise you can go spend the weekend in jail." He told me this on a Tuesday. And well, then we decided, well, we'd better get out of here, you know. And it was pretty hard to get a ride at that time of day, because after two o'clock in the morning, the only people that are on the road are policemen and truckers.

A friend of mine, my friend Beau, he's done a lot of hitching. I asked him about how much hitching he'd done, and he said, "Six thousand miles."

And I said, "You mean total?"

And he said, "No, in one trip." And so he told me if I'm ever in a situation like that, that I should go talk to the truckers, tell them that the cops are down on me and they're about to arrest me, and he said that they help you out. I haven't tried that out, so I don't know how it works.

Truck stops, places that they stop, that's another thing. You get truckers to let you off at a truck stop, you know. I haven't done the full technique with truck stops. That's supposed to be going in, you know, having a hamburger, and starting in sort of letting on where you're headed to. It's the food. It's a whole empathy thing, which I'm just starting to learn about. And the whole truck drivers' world is so different, because days of the week don't matter. And night and day they drive all the time. I don't know how many truckers do much speeding nowadays, and I'm sure there's quite a few that do. I don't see how you can drive—you can go off and drive all the way to, say, Atlantic, New Jersey and then turn around and come back without doing some speeding, even if you do take a nap or two on the way, you know, on the way back. I can't see how they could do it.

Another thing is where to stay. Sometimes you get a ride with somebody and end up going with them to stay, you know. And colleges are really good. Usually you can just walk onto a college campus, a medium-sized one. (A place like Kent, they may think that you're a fed or something.) But if you go onto a college campus, I've had people walk up to me—you've got a knapsack on your back—they walk up to you and they'll say, "Need a place to crash?" And "Have you eaten?" All this stuff. Before you know it, you've got yourself lined up with a nice piece of floor or a bed or something and food and everything else.

Or else if someone doesn't offer, you just go and ask. You get a place like that. Long-hairs with beards are a good bet, but college students in general are a pretty good bet. You can tell a lot, I mean, by looking at people, how receptive they're going to be.

Like I was saying about going to a college campus and just walking into the dining hall and getting a meal that way, you've got to be really slick about it. Well, for one thing, you find a place to put your knapsack. You've got to make yourself look like John Q. College—a student of that area—to pull it off. You've got to have a lot of gall.

What you do is: a lot of places they have numbers, students have certain numbers. And so like if you meet up with somebody, they're like a friend, they'll say, "Use a three-digit number," you know. So then you go in there, everybody walks up by the person that checks or something. But nowadays in a lot of places they have IDs that they check. Like Oberlin has IDs. What do you do there is you go in the back door and find a plate and sit down fast, you know, and things like that. Or get somebody to bring food out to you.

Hiram's is exceptionally easy. And for one thing, the guy who is head of the meal service in Hiram, I think, still thinks I'm a student there. He still feeds me every once in a while. And then, there's a guy that runs one of the cafeterias, that's a friend of mine, and he'll feed me no matter what. He'll feed me on the sly, I mean, if he had to. There's one black guy from Missouri, and his name is Mel. And so I don't really have any problem at Hiram. I could go there for ages if I wanted to.

123.

I carry a pack along and have food in it. Very seldom will I buy much of anything. I carry my cereal, which is a mixture of oats and seeds and wheat germ and stuff; and I carry along sometimes toasted soy beans, powdered milk, sort of, pretty much along that line. And then I really like, when I go across New York State, I like to have like a loaf of homemade bread and turkey and stuff, because that really goes well.

I got a ride with this one guy out in west New York State, and he was going down to Dayton, Ohio. And the next day, he was going to Alabama. And so anyways, I made up this whole-wheat spread some friend of mine made and a turkey sandwich, and I gave him one.

And I learned something with that guy: that is, I used to carry a hunting knife to cut bread with, but I don't do that anymore, because you don't want to get hit for a concealed weapon, and also it scares the hell out of a lot of people when you cut bread off with a big knife. So now I use a jackknife. I carry a jackknife.

I used to have a boy-scout jackknife. That's also public relations. You have a boy-scout jackknife, I figure, you're less likely to get busted. No kidding. Because when the policeman—you know, like I've got my hands on the car and then I say, "There's a boy-scout jackknife in my left pocket," and the policeman, in his mind, conjures up, you know, thousands of little boys, goodies, you know.

They check how sharp it is a lot of times. I haven't figured out exactly how they feel about sharpness, but basically, it's a matter of them linking up things in their minds. Why do you have the knife? What do you use it for? That type of thing. A boy-scout knife, they're not going to think of as the type of thing that you cut people up with.

I keep very close tabs on my knapsack. Like if I'm in a city, I'll put the knapsack right in the phone booth with me if I'm going to make a call. I don't like to take chances with it, because if I lose the knapsack . . . I'm learning now. What I'm going to do is I'll probably start carrying my maps in my pockets. I'd be really lost if I lost my maps—more lost than if I lost a pair of pants or food.

When you get into a car or something, don't put your knapsack all the way into the car until you're in the car yourself. And be careful when you're opening car doors that you can release your hand fast before they take off, because I've had some people, where I've gotten up just to the door, and they took off.

I've never been beaten up or anything. I've been lucky. Some friends of mine were beat up when they were just walking in Waterbury. But I've never been beaten up so far. I expect to one of these days. The only thing that's ever happened to me: I had some bottles thrown at me once, from a car. They threw one, and it hit on the pavement, and it glanced up fast, hit above my waist. But it was all flying glass, so it didn't hurt me. The next one, they tried to get me, though. They hit a sign about two feet behind me. They were really trying.

Physical harassment, you have so many things that enter into it. You have jealousy: people being jealous of you for being able to go where you want to go and not worrying about too much, because you don't have much in the way of responsibility. Also long hair gets them mad. And there are certain times when people are more polarized than they are at other times. Envy. Anger. Those are your main ones.

The other kind of harassment: the people who drive by and yell at you. But to a certain extent, one or two of those in a day, you can feel fine about. But when you get a lot of it, it can get you down.

I like hitchhiking with other people. It's nice to have somebody to talk to. It's really nice to have the company. If you're in what I consider sort of hostile areas, it's really nice to be with somebody else.

Now if you're hitching with a girl, wow! It's so easy. You just sail along it seems. You really don't care that much whether you get a ride or not. And when you're not worried about it, you get rides easier.

When I feel very unhassled, I get rides much easier. When you get scared, it's conveyed in your face, I think. Your whole being conveys it. People are animals, and they sense these things. They sense when you're scared. And when you're less hassled, people won't hassle you as much.

I use a lot more science than a lot of people do. If I'm going a long distance, I try my hardest to have a sign. And I've found the best color for signs is black letters on a yellow background. Because people think you have a sign, they think that you have more direction, you know, sort of know what you're doing more. It definitely makes it easier to get a ride, and especially if you're on a high-speed entrance or a high-speed road, if you've got a sign.

I've gotten rides with so many really nice people, really very sincere, really nice people. But you've got to remember, I'm a small-time hitchhiker compared to a lot. Plus, I haven't been through that much really rough stuff, because I'm too much of a planner when it comes to hitchhiking. Plus, well, I know my route. I mean, out to Ohio. I know everything about the route, because I've done it six times.

I call a big-time hitchhiker a one-hundred-thousand-miler. I call them big-timers, you know. That's you know, sort of my—that would be what I would—I mean, I hold a certain amount of awe of a hundred-thousand-miler. I met one once, and he was a real storyteller. Wow! He sure was. I figured on maybe fifty percent of what he said. He had these amazing stories—that he was married to four people simultaneously —I think it was four. And he picked up things when he was traveling—little balls, jacks—all kinds of little things, which he gave to the children when he went to these places. And the kids would run up to him, and they'd say, "Uncle Miles," you know, "what you got this time?" And he's just pull the stuff out of his pocket, you know. He was a real character. He was a real character.

And he said he had places to stay in every major city, which I would believe. And he probably does have places to stay everywhere. And I don't know whether he even keeps an address book. He probably just remembers. But if you've got places to stay in every major city, you have a hell of a lot of choices. You could just circulate around for a long time. Just visiting people. Nobody's going to mind, you know, you're just around for a one-night stand.

Bigtown, U.S.A.

I meet him in San Antonio, but he won't be there for long. He is a hobo. "My home is my hat," he tells me, and "don't get me mixed up with bums either." A hobo, he tells me most definitely, is not a bum. Hobos share a culture fast on the wane, sustained mainly by hobo signs—an international language of marks on trees, houses, railroad cars, and sidewalks—signs which tell other hobos everything from "stay away, the food's not good" to "watch out for railroad police." There is even a sign for generous hosts, which literally means "second helpings."

I have flown to San Antonio because it is fall, and with winter coming, he does not plan to be north or east for some time. I arrange to meet him at his hotel, on a side street in the main part of town.

San Antonio is a town of the Old West, full of adobe houses and Mexican architecture, with a picturesque winding river and gardens of desert flowers. The hotel is the kind where the Lone Ranger used to tie up Silver: wooden porch and wooden railing. I go up the steps past swinging doors and huge overhead fans with wooden blades.

The door to his room has slats at the top and a large brass handle. As I reach the door and raise my hand to knock, it opens.

"I heard you out here," he says eagerly. "I've been waiting for you." He is "Bigtown," King of the Hobos. I am surprised at his appearance. He told me on the phone he was seventy-nine, and he looks fifteen years younger. His hair is white, his skin is tan. He is wearing freshly laundered, grey workclothes and very thick-soled shoes. He is a very neat-looking hobo. He quickly explains the differences between hobos and tramps; he wants to make it clear he is no dropout; he is clearly engaged in the world. One way or another he manages to read two newspapers every day. He reads them, and he also appears in them. No sooner have I sat down than he whips out a huge scrapbook full of clippings. It is evident he regards himself as no ordinary hobo, and he wants me to know this. The scrapbook and clipping file, the eagerness for publicity have a decidedly practical function:

"That scrapbook helps me get an overcoat," he says. When Bigtown enters a town, and the charities or the rabbis or the priests or Sallies (Salvation Army) give him a hard time about getting an overcoat or whatever he needs, he has only to present his clipping file, like a portfolio, and immediately his credit is good.

He keeps calling the hotel a fleabag, but it appears to be extremely clean. Bigtown's room is equally neat. The bottles of shaving lotion, hair tonic, and other toiletries on his dresser seem to be exactly two inches apart. There is a distinctly military air to it.

He is very careful about his few possessions. His major one is a scissors sharpener, which brings him work. He carries it in an old doctor's bag he found. "I'd be lost without that," he says, leaning forward. "I sharpened the scissors of some of the most important people in the world: I sharpened Truman's scissors, Eisenhower's scissors, and Kennedy's scissors. Whenever I get to Washington, I sharpen the President's scissors. Except Nixon. I wouldn't sharpen Nixon's scissors," he says with some vehemence. His objections to Nixon are largely economic. He brings out a can of pears he recently bought to point out the price. He complains that it will be very tough to survive when a can of pears costs almost forty cents. Then he talks about the stock market. He has a passionate interest in it, and follows it closely. His ambition, had it not been for the wanderlust, would have been to be a successful businessman. He talks then about the "need to move on." He usually stays in a town a few days, but he has been here several weeks. However, he has now sharpened every pair of scissors in town and is eager to go.

When I ask him why he's moving on, he looks sad and says, "It's a sickness, this wanderlust." And then he tells me about a girl he had once, and how he "woulda liked to have kept her," but he just couldn't stay put more than eight or ten weeks at a time. That memory, however, stirs others, and he says, "Ohh, when I was young, you couldna stopped me for nothin. I had to have my women. I liked my women. Sometimes five or six times a day. I was somethin."

"How about now?"

He shrugs. "I slowed down some now," he says. "You get older, you do that less. You want to eat more. Your teeth go a little, and the price of food gets high."

He laments the demise of passenger trains, because they were, for him, the fastest way across the country. He is familiar with every bus and train connection in any part of the United States and carries thousands of timetables in his head.

His roamings have something of a tourist quality. He brings out his postcard collection, advertising "Home of the World's Largest Pecan," and "The First Bank Jesse James Robbed." He likes firsts, he says, and has a lot of those. One postcard of The Church of the Immaculate Conception in Washington, D.C. is kept, however, because they serve some of the best free food in the country.

James Gorman left home when he was sixteen and never had any urge to go back or to see his family again. When I am with him in the hotel room, he is

130.

very remote. When he calls me on the phone from Texarkana a week later, when I am in New York, he is very warm and friendly. Although it is sometimes too convenient to sum things up by linking opposites, nevertheless, I think he is closest at a distance. Running from or running toward, the miles, I suspect, are an inverse measure of his affection.

James Gorman

My hobo name's Bigtown. I got that many years ago in Seymour, Indiana, back about 1913. We was in the jungles, you know, railroad yard. Well, back in them days, they used to ship poultry in cars. That's on the Pennsylvania Railroad. And a freight train stopped there, had a poultry car on it. Man in town, he had about ten thousand chickens in them cars. We bummed him for some eggs, and he turned us down. Well, we went uptown and stole some of his chickens, and we cook em up. We had two lard cans, you know, and we cleaned them chickens so fast—one guy hole em and the other'n be pullin the feathers off. We chopped the heads off, cut the wings and legs off and gutted em and took em over by the railroad track—happened to be a waterspout there—and we washed em and cut em up and throwed em in a can to make soup and stew, stewed chicken.

We had the chicken in the water, and this guy come from uptown, and he smelled chicken, specially out in the open air, you can smell it for two or three blocks. And he got nosey. He called the law, and they put us all in jail—an old Hoosier sheriff—that's way before they had all these fingerprints and all that stuff like you got Hoover now.

We was up there two days. Had a young prosecutor, and he came in, talked to us. Couldn't identify the chickens. We done ate the biggest part of the chickens, and he couldn't find no feathers, and he couldn't find any of the guts, and he couldn't find nothin. And the sheriff, he didn't know what to do. He jus locked us up. And two days later he started askin our names. Everybody give him a name, all phony names, different towns and everything. He got down to me, and I give im my right name, where I was born at. And he says, "Oh, you're from the bigtown," he says. "You're a smart guy." And all the guys start laughin. "I ship hogs there," he says, "St. Louis." That's how I got that name.

A hobo works. He's got somethin to do. He peddles somethin. Old hobo Benson, he used to be aroun New York, aroun Macy's. He used to have that *Hobo News,* an he used to peddle that paper. They're sign painters. They'll do everything. For years I pushed lawnmowers. I sold needle books after World War Two, German needle books. I bought em for fifteen cents and sell em for fifty cents, three for a buck. An don't think these women didn't buy em, specially in these small towns. Now, you can't get no hundred an twenty-five needles for fifty cents.

I sharpen scissors now for a livin. Sharpen clippers an I sharpen knives. I sharpen scissors or an ordinary housewife's knife, it'll last her a year. Same with scissors.

I keep clean. I'm one of the very few that don't drink or smoke. I don't even drink that lousy coffee. I eat, oh, anything I can get that's halfway decent. Meat's about a thing a the past, it's so high. An San Antonio, this is the lousiest town in the United States to get any decent food, these Mexican restaurants.

A hobo's life today is gettin rough. Years ago we had so many places to get in, you understan. They're all gone. No more passenger trains. There's very few passenger trains left anymore. You go into a railroad yard now, an all you see is a bunch of weeds.

Oh man, I rode freight trains. That's all you can ride now. When I first started out, a thirty-four foot boxcar. Now the smallest boxcar they got today is about sixty foot. An they got all what they call piggy-backs—put them tracks on top of these flat cars. The wind, it'll whip you to death. The damn things go sixty miles an hour, you got no protection. Now all the new boxcars comin out have doors like the refrigerators have. You see a refrigerator, they got that bar goes across, goes down to the bottom, up to the top. Well, you can't get into them cars anymore. The only place you got now is an empty coal car or a flat car with the sides on it to ship steel. Or get in the back unit of the diesel. Everything's changed. You're livin in a new world.

An this housin. I tell you it's murder to get a place to stay. Jails are open—if you can get to em. You can sleep in the jails all over the United States. Here, you come in this town destitute, you go down to that police—they got one jail in this town. Police, they take you down to Salvation Army; they give you one night over there every ninety days. That's no good.

Salvation Army, they're the biggest racketeers in the world. They're

133.

listed on Wall Street—American Salvage's the name they're listed under. I don't know how many millions—Salvation Army, it's a name. They're all over the world, but they operate different. This is the lousiest place of all their operations, is in the United States.

People who go to Salvation Army, we call em Sallies. They're lazy, they're winos, you understan. They're helpless, ain't got no ambition. We call that religion ear-beatin. You know, that's that same old stuff, jus like some Sears'n Roebuck preachers, they give you the same thing, one theme song, John 3:16. You get that every day. Oh, it's murder.

I don't believe in God. The man's been dead I don't know how many years. They're sending them astronauts up there, an they never seen nobody up there. But I don't argue about it, cause I don't know.

I ain't never been on no welfare. I don't get nothin from social security. Here's my social security here. I bought this thing out in Boise, Idaho fifteen years ago for half a buck, this doctor's bag.

You carry this all day long—it's fifteen pounds—I can knock you through that door over there. I ain't gonna do it. I take care of myself. I don't abuse myself. The only bad habit I got—I'm gonna tell you straight from the shoulder—I'm gettin so old now it don't bother me like it used to: when I was young, romance, whew! I couldn't get enough of it. Two or three times a day if I could get it. I'm very polite aroun women, polite as a preacher. I let em proposition me. I never turn em down. But who's gonna marry me? I wouldn't stay put. This is kinda a record for me—three months here in one spot. I'm gettin ready to leave now.

I made six dollars this mornin sharpening knives. I go to beauty shops, barber shops, tailor shops. Charge fifty, seventy-five, and one dollar here. But when I get back East, it's a buck. You gotta get that dollar, you can't live. You hit New York an try to live on two, three dollars a day, an see how far you get.

Nineteen-oh-eight, jus like any other nutty kid, jus run off from home. I went over the river from St. Louis to east St. Louis an caught a freight train. I finally went up to—oh, about eighty mile from St. Louis. I slept in the jail over there that night. They want to know where my home was—you know how police are. I wouldn't tell em nothin. So they turn me out the next day. Oh, I got another train, finally went up

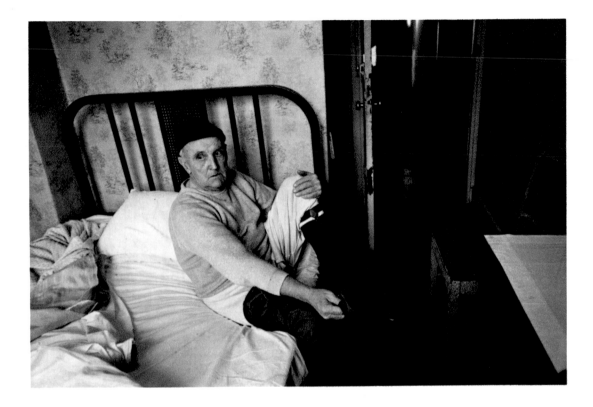

to Chicago. I didn't know nothin bout railroads in them day. I jus went on one an stayed with it. I got hungry, I went begged in the houses. You get hungry, you'll ask for somethin, don't worry about that. Ask for little jobs, odd jobs.

Back in them days you had stores, them stores'd feed you. Today they got chain stores, they don't give you nothin. They won't give you the dirt off the floor. Them managers in them stores, they get a big salary'n they get a commission; an then the're gonna jeopardize their job, an I don't blame em a bit. Oh, the independent merchants'd take care of you. The Church feed you, give you a meal ticket. Then you didn't have all these rackets you got today, these Salvation Armies, the best thing you can do is get some kinda job where you can support yourself.

Years ago I sold lead pencils. I used to use them to beg with more than anything else. You had a potential sale anyplace you went down the street. That's before these ballpoint things come out. I sold six for a quarter, I made eighteen cents profit, made four or five sales a day, you live all day. I put the riggin on people, means jus like beggin. I bummed one of the most prominent men in the United States in Washington, D.C.

I'm on Connecticut Avenue in the evenin, warm weather—can't do that in the wintertime, they're all buttoned up an they got their gloves on. This man took me down the Elks Club an paid a month's room rent, then took me to a nice restaurant, gave me about eight meal tickets for about five dollars apiece. He didn't give me no cash. You know who he was? This man is dead today. He was United States Senator Peter Gary from Rhode Island. That's the honest truth.

But the best thing that ever happened in my days as a hobo, sixty-five years this comin June, is the laundrymats. If you can't get enough money to wash your clothes in the laundrymats, then you're helpless.

These shirt and pants, this is Lee. They cost fifteen dollars. I use two washers and one dryer. I got enough socks to put on clean socks every day. I gotta keep clean, cause I go in businesses, I go in hospitals, I go in doctors' offices.

November and December for my business is murder. The people got one thing on their mind: Christmas. I generally wind up here in San Antonio every year in October. Last year I picked up five hundred dollars before Christmas. But two winos got in ahead of me this year, and they ruined me. They went into these shoppin centers, beauty salons, sharpenin blades. They'll do everything, but all they can do is sharpen scissors. Can't sharpen knives, can't sharpen clippers.

Today you got hippies beggin along the streets. You got girls, hippie girls, beggin. I can't figure em out. I think the war's the cause of it. Every one of them bastards got good-lookin girls. I mean, nice girls. How do they get in that shape? Look at their clothes. They're nasty, they're dirty.

These guys today are hitchhikers. I wouldn't get three feet on the highway. I ain't gonna get on the highway. I get these buses goin short jumps. On long jumps I catch the IC, go to Central Illinois, Illinois Central jus merged with another railroad now. Maybe it was the M & O. Starts in New Orleans an ends up in Minnesota.

You know another hobo jus as soon as he opens his mouth, starts talkin. I got four, five thousand words, hobo words. A wingy's a guy who's only got one arm. A dingy's a drunk, years ago. And plingy's—I don't know what that plingy is. Probably some other spook.

See, I talk to the railroad man. A hoger's an engineer. H-O-G-E. You got a singer, that's the brakeman; railroad bull—we call em different things—that's railroad detectives. They don't need em anymore. These fast freight trains pull in right on the main line; in fifteen minutes they're gone.

I'll catch the SP outta here, Southern Pacific. I know what time these trains leave or I find out. I'll go in the yard office, and they all know me, my God, sure.

You go into the yard, ask the yard inspector if they're any shorts goin out—a train comes in an picks up some cars, understan—they'll all tell you. You start speakin their language, they know what you're talkin about. Lots a times I get talkin to the conductor, I get back an ride in the caboose. They don't bother you anymore, not like they used to.

I used to cook right alongside the road. Fresh meat, boiled eggs and toast, put it in the skillet. We used to go out an look for dry wood. In the jungles we had pots an pans. Today they got these new skillets, electric skillets they got now, you can cook a meal in em. You gotta have a electric cord about one hundred fifty, two hundred feet long. You get around these railroad yards, where you get a plug like that, put in there, you're in there thirty minutes, you got your food cooked an you're gone.

142.

Cookin over a fire, that's obsolete, you understan. The old wood is wet, you gotta look for all that, pans get smoky. These electric skillets.

The old-time hobos, they use a pot or a skillet, they clean em for the guys behind. A tradition, you understan. But that's gone.

The way I operate: you can't stay out in the wintertime no more. No more depots. They have a train goes through a town, the agent gets there one hour before arrival, an one hour after a train leaves, they lock it up. You gotta look for housing. So now I'm headin for New Orleans. Stay there till the first of March, first of April. Then straight north on the IC. Get up aroun Springfield or Champaign an turn east. I'll go in Indianapolis maybe couple days, go into Columbus, then Pittsburgh. Well, I'll go way into Pennsylvania, way up aroun Scranton, Wilkes-Barre, Allentown. Pennsylvania, they got all them missions up there. They're clean. You got places to stay there, and there's money in Pennsylvania. There's more money in one foot of Pennsylvania than there is down here in a square mile. Go up to Britt for the first of August, hobo convention, that's right. Then I can't tell—might go to the West Coast—can't tell nothin about me. I won't come back here no more. They got this five-cent sales tax in this state.

I been to Canada, been to Mexico. I been in all the provinces of Canada. United States, forty-eight states, but not the two new ones, cause the only way to get there is by air. I never flew in my life.

American cities, they're all about the same. The buses are painted different, that's about all. The police cars are painted different colors.

I don't like California. There's too many niggers out there. World War Two, these niggers all down here in the South. They don't need em anymore on these cotton plantations, and World War Two, Chrysler brought em out there by the shiploads, workin on some shipyards. They seen California, an they liked the climate, so they stayed there. That's the reason they have that trouble in Frisco, them nigger preachers. Ever since the Republicans get back in power, they stop that real fast. Reagan. They got eighteen, nineteen million people in California. I don't know how many million they got on relief out there.

143.

I don't hate em. Got nothin against em cept they're dangerous, understan. They're hungry, they're desperate, they ain't got no money, they'll knock you on the head an rob you.

Like these kids now in these railroad yards, they throw rocks at you. These winos, they try to rob you. I carry a gas gun with me—one of them things you shoot right in their face, the women carry em in their purses. It's a mace of some kind. The only thing you gotta watch is the way the wind is blowin, it don't blow back into you, you understan.

I know every town in the United States. Any town with five thousand population, I know where it's at, what's in there.

My home's under my hat. I don't have no trouble. I'm just lucky.

I read the newspapers every day. That's my education. Can't even interpret a lotta the words. Can't even pronounce em. I get the idea. I watch the market. If I had money, I woulda been a multi-millionaire. This is a good country. It's not the country needs reformin. It's the way people are robbin it blind.

Plainfield, New Jersey

The sense of a large society gone awry, of the great wrongness of social development, sits like a weight on this factory town. In the locally staffed community office, when a woman comes in desperate for a job and is told by a diffident receptionist, "Idonhaveanythingrightnowcomebacknextweekfileanapplicationandicallyou," local staffing seems to solve nothing. She may as well be at IBM. There is not much hope of solving things in this place. Racial tensions have been high for the last years, white cops shot, black youths killed. The biggest factory closed down last year, forcing many white workers to make their first appearances at the welfare office in the black part of town. At such a time the black welfare officers gloat: "Now you know how it feels."

The biggest advertisements seem to suggest nothing so much as a decrepit body in need of repair: Optometrist, Hearing Aids, Surgical Supplies. Inside the community office there is another kind of ad for a huge record album called "The American Family Guide to Drug Abuse," in red, white, and blue colors. There are four LP records, the album says, for only nine dollars.

The day I am to be taken on a tour of the heart of the ghetto of this town, I am with two black women who grew up here. We stop at the black newspaper office, where a typewriter has been stolen, and the editor says, "Irene, you get the word out I want my electric typewriter back."

Irene says okay, and we get back in the car.

"Where are we going?" I ask.

"To the corner to see if we can get that typewriter back."

"The corner?"

"Yes. If you're white you go to the cops, if you're black you go to the corner."

We go several blocks down the street to some low income projects, in front of which are about thirty men sitting on the stoops and standing around. The car pulls up, and Irene leans out the window to one of them and says, "Hey, Eddie says put the word out, he wants his typewriter back. He means it. He's gonna put some hard talkin on you if he don't see it."

"If he don't *see* it?" a young man says, shaking his head, "When they take it?"

"Last night."

"Last night?" the young man hits his head, "well now, if he don't know where it is now, he ain't never gonna know where it is. That's goooooone." And he makes a long sliding motion with his hands.

We get out of the car and walk down the block. The men are lounging and at ease. The girls who pass by are sassy in leather vests and hot pants. Then comes Rita, in white vinyl boots, a red dress that barely covers her ass, and a white peroxided Afro that is nearly out to her elbows. Her eyelashes are at least four inches long, and she clanks a lot. Eight bracelets fall up and down her arm as she swirls her hands in the air. Rita is a spectacle, and she knows it.

"When Mama says she goin out, she goin out," she says, shaking her behind as she comes near us. "I tole my man, I said, now I got to go make me some frens, and you know you can do it. Uh-hun. You must make sure that he know you ain't lookin for a home, and he ain't lookin for a home, why there ain't no natural reason you can't make some frens." She keeps flicking her leg so her knee locks, and this combines with the ass movement to make up what came close to a bump and grind. At the same time she stares past us toward a group of men, talking loudly about how much they want to see "it." She says, "Thas the only reason you sittin on the curb, don I know it, so you can see up my dress." She flounces a little as she says this, smoothing her dress. She seems immensely proud of what she has under it, and the rest of the afternoon, which she spends with us, she keeps offering up her own brand of homespun advice: "You better use what your mama gave you. Ain't gonna improve it if you don use it," and "Most women stupid if you ast me. With what they got they can do anythin they want. Anythin. Only reason they ain't got what they want is they're stupid."

Rita works as a waitress when she can find work, but it's hard to find because of her unconventional looks. She does not worry, she says, because when "everythin is everythin,"

"When what?" I say.

"When everythin is everythin," Rita says, "I'm gonna have two cars, a big house and a garage and private school for my children. Get out of this dump."

"When everythin is everythin." Some day.

Chico's movements are quick and graceful. His speaking voice would have to be scored, so full of innuendo, rhythm, and pitch is it when he says, "Heyyyy baby, everythinnns coooool," bending back into his waist, moving his arm wide and free, always swinging from some invisible spring where his spine should be. You wonder at all that life, that energy; how does he contain it?

When I first met Chico he was on the street. He was graceful, happy, excited, at ease. The second time I call to meet him, he asks me to meet him at his house.

Chico's family consists of twelve children. They live in a pleasant, well-furnished home on a tree-lined street. His father is a musician, has built his own boat, and seems to be a man of many talents. His mother is elegant, soft-spoken, and graceful. The family is polite and cordial to me and Bruce, although they have every reason to be suspicious, since we are white and did meet Chico on the street. His parents clearly do not like Chico's "street life." When I remark to Chico that no other member of his family talks as he does, with a certain hipster quality, he points out that he is the only one in his family who feels an attraction to "the street." He loves the movement and excitement of it, and mostly the sociability. He clearly is a young man who loves company.

When Chico's mother reads the transcripts of the tapes, she is surprised and angry. She tells me she thinks the tapes make him sound like a hoodlum, some uneducated person, and I can see from her point of view why she thinks that. Chico does not talk or sound like any typical middle-class person. He has too much imagination, feeling, and style to accept any convention; and one of the ways he expresses this is how he talks. He is a natural actor, and he loves talking. He does this with so much humor and style, no matter what he says, it seems to be always bordering on both philosophy and entertainment.

Chico calls his girl friend over because Bruce wants to take pictures. She is a refined, regal-looking girl. Her name is Classie Mae. I ask her what she will do about a job. She is not yet twenty and doesn't seem to know. There really are no jobs in this outlying suburb of New York. Ambition is a strange word. For what is there to be in this place? What is there to aspire to? The people I meet who have the good jobs, all federal programs of some sort, communicate a sense of futility about any change in things, and I wonder what is there here for Chico?

It is part of our social dilemma that there exist no institutional structures to channel and direct his kind of feeling and imagination. Of course he has a few more years on parole, but he is extraordinary in his intelligence as well as his honesty;

yet his only opportunity at the moment seems to be his job waxing floors. Now, it doesn't matter. With such spirit and energy, youth is his biggest asset, and it seems to need no justification other than that it is a time in one's life. But later, I wonder, what happens later?

Chico's job is his insurance; he does not want any more trouble with the police, but he wants to be on the street. He works from nine at night until nine in the morning, and then when he walks down the street at nine-thirty in the morning, just coming from the job, a police car pulls over. He is not with a friend, so the police cannot run him in as they have done before for "consorting with a known criminal." ("Known criminal?" Chico cries. "Everybody on this block's a known criminal. Everybody been busted for somethin. You got to walk alone or be hauled in.") He knows there's nothing they can get him for, and yet the cop beckons. Chico walks to the police car.

"We're taking you in," the cop says.

"What for?" Chico says.

"Those gloves in your pocket."

"These gloves?" Chico reaches to his back pocket for the gloves he uses to hold the floor waxer.

"Possession of burglary tools," the cop says, and Chico is furious at them, at himself, at the paranoia it would require for him to have been able to anticipate that. Chico must be careful because he is on parole, but as he says, "How careful can you be and live?"

His gloves snap the car seat. His girl hums in the back. Bruce is driving. I sit in front. Suddenly I hear Classie Mae whisper to Chico, "We have to go there," and he asks us to stop off so she can pick up some money for a job he got painting somebody's living room. The girl runs out of the car, up to a house. In a minute she is back saying, "She says she's only got a fifty-dollar bill. Have we got change?"

Chico is furious. "Las week she only had change for a hundred-dollar bill. She knows I can't change that. Shit!"

I am going on a trip and have just cashed an expense check. "I have change for fifty dollars," I say.

"Ohhh, wait til she see that, just wait!" Chico slaps his leg, his girl runs from the car.

"She must know how to play to win," I say, "a hundred-dollar bill last week, a fifty this."

"She ain't *playin* them numbers," Chico says, setting me straight. "Noo, nooo, she's runnin the numbers." It's a strange world of small illegalities, big monies, expensive tastes, and provincial experience.

As we drive down the street, Chico points out, "Thas the corner, thas where he got shot." That afternoon someone was murdered on that corner; two of Chico's friends who were there were arrested. "Ummm hmmmm," Chico looks worried, "if you hadn't come out, you know, if we weren't drivin aroun, I woulda been there, standin right there, man."

Chico Brown

I can't dig cooped up, bein'n that house. It jus gives me a feelin —it's not my thing, bein'n house, jus sitting out watchin television, readin a newspaper, listenin to the radio, to the record player. I can do that shit in the street. I can listen to radio, walk up an down the street, talk to anybody I want, still got my radio. I wanna television, I can do that, too. But bein in that house—you go'n the house when it's time to go to bed, when you wanna go get somethin to eat. Or if you jus feel like layin down an bein by yourself, go in the house.

I don like bein by myself. I'm gonna tell ya, I don dig bein alone. No sir. Um-um. Bein alone. Man's a fool that wanna be alone. Can't do nothin bein alone. Sure, it's cool to be alone when you wanna work out a problem. An then, you can't work it out without somebody bein there. You understan what I'm sayin? You got to have somebody to help you succeed in what you gonna do. So bein alone: people tell me, "I jus wanna be alone." *You* go ahead. You go sit in the corner, in the backyard, even in the street, if you wanna. Don mean nothin to me. I'm not gonna be by myself, long as there's somebody to talk to. I wouldn't care if he's yellow, I'm gonna be with im. Don make no difference to me what he is, what he do, what anything. He can be a criminal, he can be the President, if the man suits ma taste, we gonna do it, no matter what it be. I don care where he is.

An you find some people say, "Man, you shouldn't be with that girl. She's so an so an so an so." Well, I don wanna hear that shit. Let *me* find out. Yeah. Well, you find all kind a people like that. An you get people like that, they envy other people. Thas why you got so much motherfuckin gossip out there, because people can't dig where other people comin from. If they'd sit down once in a while, try to figure out why this guy's doin this, why she's doin that, they might comprehend what everybody else is tryin to do. But not. First anyone comes out their mouth, I'm on for poor. Pshew. "He ain't where it at." Why? Because he ain't doin what you want to do? There's all kind a people like that. I met em all when I went to Bordentown. Boy, thas where you meet all kinda people, down'n that penitentiary. Yup. All walks of life.

I went down there in the first part of January. Fifteenth. I went down there for a larceny an a violation of probation. On probation for possession of marijuana. They call it a narcotic. But it ain't a narcotic. Don care what they say.

After that I was three years' probation. Why, that was cool. So that went on for about a year. I stayed on probation. Then I started messin aroun, I started messin aroun, an messin aroun. An then I wouldn't go see the man anymore, cause I tired of him askin me the same ole bullshit. I didn't wanna hear that: "What you been doin? You been a good kid out there in the street, man? Ain't gettin in no trouble, are you? You go anywhere?"

"No. I ain't got no job. No, I am not bein good." Jus don be askin me all them questions. To me "bein good" must mean stayin outta trouble. I don know. You can stay on the street an be outta trouble. I'm doin it now. If you want to. You understan? Only if you want to. Not hard. Nope. Like I say, you do what you wanna do. Ain't nobody makin you do nothin. If you wanna steal somethin, you steal it because you want it. If you wanna jump on somebody, you do because you want to.

Needin to. Thas a different story there. I ain't got nothin to say against them people. Boy, when you need somethin, you gonna git it. You don care how you git it. There ain't nobody gonna stan in your way. I never been in that category. Though I was surenough out, when I was out there, I jus had to go out there an take somethin from somebody.

But I know an I've seen dudes that I hung out with, they surenough sayin, "Man, I don know what I'm gonna do. Ain't got no money, an I ain't got no job, an damn if I'm gonna be broke." An there it is. "I'll be back."

"Where you goin?"

"I gotta go take off somethin"—take somethin from somebody, somebody's house, money, store, anything. You know.

An then, you got them guys out there who do it jus for the hell of it. They don need it. I was one of them. I ain't have to go out there an steal. For what? You seen my people. I can get anything I want. I don want nothin from them. But I'm gonna get it on my own.

You really wanna know how old I was when I started this? You really wanna know the truth? I's about ten or eleven. I's hanging out there in the barber shop. Pshew. Boy, I learn a lot down in that barber shop. Thas where I learn how to cut hair an shit like that. Guys there was much older than me. An I used to be sittin down listenin to em. You know. An you know, bein a kid then, you hear dudes about twenty-twenty-one years ole talkin, a lot of shit goin on, fillin your head up. An plus the crew I was runnin with at that time, they's pretty mean.

Like a dude go out there an had stold somethin, an had stuck up somethin, an took this from somebody. An they been out with this woman an that woman an what they did to her, what they did to her. Boy, I was sittin down there an my ears get big when I hear shit like that. Cause I'd be thinkin, man, if he can do it, whas stoppin me from doin it? You know, same thing, you know.

Ain't even phase me think it bein wrong. Shit. Ain't never crossed my mind nothin bein wrong. I'd a been surenough dead if it done. Jus like when I started shootin dope. Now, you know, boy, you mess aroun too much with your dope, you gonna die. Think I thought about that? Pshew. It don bother you. You see, when you out there doin wrong, you don even worry bout whas gonna happen to you until it happen. An then you worry about it. Until then, thas the las thing in your mind.

An you don think about funny-kind-of-shit whas gonna happen to you until it happens, an then when it happens, you figure how you gonna git out of it.

First time I stole? I don know. Think I was downtown. Think I stole some toy an got killed for stealin it, too. Tole my mama. She beat the shit outta me. She beat the shit outta me, boy. She—pshew. "If this what's gonna happen, I ain't tellin no more." Boy, she beat the shit outta me. Boy. I say, "God damn." I wanted it an she wouldn't buy it.

"Ha!" She seen me with that toy. "Where you git that from? Who gave you the money?"

"I-I-I"

"What? You lyin."

Boy, I got my ass whipped. I never forget that. She beat the shit outta me. Almos made me not want to steal no more.

Like I said, crew I was with, they was mean. They was bout fifteen of them. Boy, we did little bit of everything. Dudes I was with, I'd say only one, one, ain't never been to jail. Knock on wood, I was the las one to go, too. All them got busted up in Allendale and Jamesburg. My feet was just a little too fast for em. An shit, when it get hot, I know how to get on the way. Run. Get on the way. You understan?

Like I say, you out to do wrong, you got to have good head an you got to have good feet. You can't have one or the other. You got to have both. Know when it time for you to split an know when it time for you not to. An you can't have a shaky body, be worried whas gonna happen if you out there stealin, if you out there rippin off somebody. You can't think what if, cause you don know whas gonna happen until it's time to come up to you to face it.

Cops don bother me much now. But when I first came home, I'm suckin it there. An when I first come home off that other thing, wow! Boy, I caught natural born hell behind that.

Like I can't walk down the street with nobody on parole. I can't walk down the street with my younger brother. Cause thas bein—they got some ole kinda term downtown they use—consortin, there it is, with a known criminal. Thas bullshit. Now thas a whole lot of bullshit. How you gonna tell me I can't walk down the street with this man cause he been in jail? What that got to do with it? Yeah. Consortin with a known criminal. I look at em like they're crazy, cause they crazy to me. They got to be mad.

But anyway, it all boils down to the same thing: people quit fuckin with people all the time, an then people go ahead an do what they gotta do, this'd be a whole lot better place to live in, you know. Sure, you gotta have law an order for people thas gonna go out there an hurt other people, you know, an be takin peoples' shit. Because without the po-lice, this'd be a hell of a town, you know. Everybody'd have to be worryin bout was gonna be happenin next.

But I say, if you see a man smokin a reefer, thas his business. What you got to do with it? You ain't got to smoke it if you don wanna. If you see a man out there shootin dope, thas his business. You ain't gotta do it cause he's doin it. So leave im alone. He ain't botherin you. Man want to go out an drink wine, thas his business. He wanna drink liquor, thas his business. If he wanna run down the street stark naked, thas his motherfuckin business. But you got people that see you doin somethin an to them it's wrong, an why? Because you say it's wrong, so it's got to be wrong, cause I'm doin it. Cause you don do it.

Here in this town everything revolves aroun Liberty Street. No matter where you go in Plainfield, no matter who you know in Plainfield, sooner or later, they be down on Liberty Street. For what or for who don make no difference. But if you want somethin, if you need somebody, or if you lookin for somebody, you find em on Liberty Street.

Jus bein in that street is home to me. I can do what I want out there. I can get anything. I don want for nothin when I'm out there. Anything. Anything I want, I can get it right out there. No matter what it is. I don care what it is, I'll get it. It could be—I don know. Now, man, I don care where it come from, Chico find it. I know all kinda people.

It all depends on the mood you be in. Let's say I want to get high. I go'n get high. If I want a drink, I go get the drink. I want some more dope, I go out there an get that, too. Not shootin stuff. Thas a hassle. Shootin stuff is a hassle, boy, cause it keep you runnin all the time. You ain't got time for nothin else. I found out me an dope don get along.

Music? That *is*. Thas finger poppin. Thas all I do, jus listen radio. All day long. Got to have radio playin. Otherwise, television nighttime. Cause it ain't nothin good in the daytime.

Women? Scuse me ma expression, but youall a drag. Youall a pain in the neck. Serious. Youalls a real pain in the neck. Boy, youall go through all kinda shit. An what bugs me the most about youall—WOMEN—it's all right for youall to talk to a boy, but God damn, let me talk to a girl. I got to be doin this, or I got to be doin—an all I said was "Hello." It's all right for you to turn your head an say, "Man, he sure is cute." But let me say it: "Man, that hole's sure fine," I got a lotta shit from youall. Thas why I can't be tight up with one woman.

Women they cool. I love to be with em. Don make no difference what they is, they all right with me. But no matter what she is or where she come from or what she may have, she's cool long as she stay in her place. In her place: leavin me

157.

alone an don try to be gettin in ma motherfuckin business. An tryin to be nosy an figure out what I'm gonna do or where I'm goin or who I'm gonna be with.

Men sharin chores don bother me, cause I feel as though thas what they wanna do, let em do it. They ain't hurtin me, you know. She says, "Do the dishes," do em. Ain't gonna kill you. That ain't gonna kill you. I look at it this way: if she can do the dishes, motherfucker, you can wash em too. Masculinity? What that got to do with it? That don have a goddamned thing to do with it, any masculinity. Get your ass over there an wash em dishes. If it come up to go to the motherfuckin laundromat, take the clothes an go to the laundromat. If it calls for em to clean up the house, clean up the damn house. Because if you don have no broad, you understan, you'd do it anyway.

All day long you sit on your ass, don do nothin when you go to work. You don do a goddamned thing when you go to work no way. Eight hours. I feel as though household work is harder than goin to work. You understan? Thas my point. All that dustin, all that shit you got to pick, specially if you got kids, you know, three or four kids. You got to clean up after them constantly—not five, ten minutes—constantly. You got to pick up this. He done broke somethin. Junior knocked over the food outta the ice box. Sally done fucked up the bathroom. Gettin them downstairs. They'll pull the windowshade off. You got to *do*. Ma's got to be ping, ping, ping. An what he doin? Sittin there, if he got a desk job, writin, or if he be in the factory, fuckin with the fellas. You understan me?

Only thing I don dig bout goin to work is gettin up early in the mornin an punchin that clock. I don dig it. I jus don dig it. Now I go to work now. I always go to work, but I don dig goin to work, an I don have to go to work, cause I can make jus as much money out there in the street. Matter of fact, I can make more money out there in the street than I can make doin a day job durin the week—a whole lot more money, cause I've done it many a day. Say you make twenty-five dollars now. I can go out there now an make a hundred. An it won't take me eight hours. It won't even take me a good two hours. You understan what I'm sayin?

So I know I don have to go to work. Don have to swipe somethin an sell it. Don have to do that. I can jus talk to some people an get their money from em. Jus talk to some people. But it all boils down to who you talkin to, what you know about the street. An me, I know too much. I been out there all my life, ever since I was ten I been out there.

Jus like, say, me an you sittin here talkin, right? An we'd be rappin an rappin, jus go ahead rappin, talkin bout a little bit of everythin. An then we jump into this conversation. I know you got big bucks. I ain't got a dime in my pocket. I got to get this sucker to give me that money. Not all of it. Maybe ten or fifteen dollars. An you figure, if I can get ten or fifteen dollars from four people, thas doin good, an doin it sittin down talkin.

Or then I can go out there, if I wanted, sellin dope. An I know the dudes out there sellin dope makin big bucks. You hear me? Make big money. Not that bullshit ten or fifteen dollars. I know dudes out there makin two hundred, three hundred dollars a night, jus by sellin dope.

Know dudes out there gamblin. I gambled good as I wanna be, specially with the dice. Shit. Won a good bit. I don dig gamblin. I got a thing about givin my money. I ain't givin away nothin. I'm tellin you. An gamblin, I hate the dudes, but I can gamble good.

See, I put a limit on my gamblin. If I take a hundred dollars with me an win two hundred dollars, I'm quittin. I got three hundred dollars. I'm not goin to try to get that other five hundred dollars on the table, cause you're not gonna get it, if thas what you got six or seven feet in front of you, you're not gonna get all the money. Very seldom you have somebody thas gonna win all the money, unless he put the cheat on you. An then you got to have a hell of an eye to watch them dice. So when you gamble with the dice, you got to put a limit. You take a hundred dollars win or lose. Thas where you go into debt. Take a hundred, lose a hundred, you quit. You don go back in your pocket no more. Sometime you'll hear other people say, "Damn, I lost a hundred dollars. I gotta try to get it back." You'll never git it back. Very seldom a dude git back, he losin money. He lose the rest of it. You take that hundred dollars if you lose, "I got to go. See youall." Take that hundred dollars if you win, "I got to go, see youall." The same thing.

If I could sit down an really tell you about me, you'd think I was crazy. Lemme tell you, I'm sposed to be dead by now, the shit I have been through. Like ma mother tell me, she says, "I'm surprised. I thought you'd be dead long time ago."

"Ah, ma. Don worry bout this son. He know what he doin."

Don know shit. Just gettin way by the skin of ma teeth. What she's mainly worried about: I used to be a hell of a fighter—street fighter. Hell of a street fighter. I member many a night when I come home all cut up. Pshew. Knocked all up.

Not scared. You be nervous fore it happened, but soon as it happened, jus get home, cause all you worried bout now is whas gonna happen to you. I know many days I come home, tried to get past em, an had blood like up my arm or I'd a been all cut up, blood on ma head, tryin a sneak in the house. Pshew. Then get all bandaged up. An she's bustlin:

"What happened to you?"

"Nothin."

"Don't tell me that shit. Well, how come?"

"I fell." My favorite story. "I fell." Ain't fell no more'n the man'n the moon a fell outta the sky. Come in here, face be cut up, hand be all bruised up:

"Why your hand like that?"

"Oh, I was down the team center punchin on the big bag."

Knowin I'd done somethin. Man, she know I'm lyin. But I jus can't figure out to tell her. I don known what I've been doin, because, really, to me she bein nosy anyway. Everybody says, "You mother, she got a right to know." But to me she's bein nosy. Now, I feel more hurt if she didn't ask me. If I come in the house all cut up, jus walk by, she don say nothin. "God damn. Whas wrong with mom? She don care?" I don know. It boils all down. Shit. Ah. This life is a hell of a thing. But it's wonderful.

Life is the beautiful thing in the world. It's so complicated, so fucked up, that even if you look at it from the fucked-up side, it's still good.

That bullshit: "You go to heaven," it's a goddamn lie. God? Me. Me. I am God. Cause you hear that bullshit, "When you die, you go to heaven. The angels come back an git you, right? It's a goddamn lie. When you die, your ass be down in that ground. The worms eat you ass up. You ain't goin nowhere. You understan me? When you put up under there, you stay there. You ain't goin nowhere. When you get down there in this hard concrete shit, how the hell you gonna get out? Now, you tell me.

Spirit. Soul. Dig that. Your spirit an your soul. If thas what it takes for to go to heaven or hell, don take me. Cause it can't be no worse than where I'm livin. It can't be no worser, it can't be no harder, it can't be no rougher. Talk that bullshit. If there was anything as heaven, I ain't goin. Cause damn if I was good. I ain't never gonna be good. An if God gonna forgive me, he got a lotta forgivin a do.

That politics shit, it don interest me. I wouldn't care who be mayor; I wouldn't care if they ain't have no mayor. I wouldn't care if they ain't have no councilmen. Leave me alone. If you want to worry about other folkes, what other folkes is doin, you worry bout it. You man. Knowin that ole bullshit up in city hall, it's crooked. An you can't sit here an tell me it ain't. Nobody else gonna sit here an tell me it ain't. Them folks is crooked.

Now, they work, they got a job, too, right? Well, they beatin people outta they money, puttin in they pocket, jus like I'm out here beatin people, puttin that money in ma pocket. Everybody's beatin somebody, cause you can see it.

"Man, what you gone done?"

Bust his big guinea ass, takin money outta the contracts for buildings.

Now, you know, you look at it an say, "Now it's politics," an "this is war," an all that. "Government done gave such an such—government gone gave ten thousand dollar for an anti-drug program." You believe it. If he gave ten thousand, he's gonna get thirty thousand back. Believe me. He's not gonna give you ten thousand dollars for nothin. You not gonna give nobody ten thousand dollars for nothin unless some good gonna come out of it for you. An you figure, he gonna give ten thousand dollars for the Urban Coalition or things, for anti-drug programs, for the rat control shit, an all that bullshit. He givin all that money, right? Jus givin that money out. Why given that money? Cause he wanna stop em drugs, he wanna help the poor people, he wanna control that bullshit. Sure. He wanna help em. I grant you that. But in the meantime, while he's helpin, there's some kind of way hooked up for more money to be comin back.

Cause if you got big money, big money always makes more money. Jus like if you got a dollar an you know how to use that dollar, you can use that dollar, make you five dollars. Make you five, make you ten. An so on. You understan me? So if they got ten million dollar, believe me, they takin that ten an gonna make twenty more for it. They ain't givin it away. Givin it away! Look at it this way: if they gonna give way all that motherfuckin money, this country wouldn't be shit. Now, would it? All them federal grants. All that money for this an that.

Jus like in Chicago, they gave that gang—well, God damn, cause the gang was raisin so much hell in Chicago, because they ain't have nothin, government gave em, I think it was close to a million dollars. You know what that gang was doin with that money? Spendin it up between theyselve. The government gave em money—not all at

163.

one time—they was givin it to the leader of the gang. Shit. That motherfucker was buyin cars, buyin everything. Thas where they messed up there. Thas just what they did—jus gave them the money. Read it in the *Life* magazine while I's in penitentiary. They didn't give em all the money at one time. They gave em so much of the money to start this program. They started the program, right. Keep that front up. In the meantime, in the front of the house it was Program, in the back of the house, it was spend that money right on up.

They ain't givin away nothin, cause there ain't nobody givin away nothin, nothin.

It's a big ole circle. There's a whole bunch of numbers in it. You got a number. I got a number. An one day that ball is gonna be spinnin an spinnin an spinnin an keep on spinnin. An then it stop. An you number twelve. An number come up. It's over. You understan me?

Whas gonna happen tomorrow is gonna happen. An whas gonna happen the day after tomorrow is gonna happen. Ain't no use sittin here sayin, "Tomorrow I'm gonna go out there, I'm gonna make this an this." Thas just a goddamn lie. A whole lot of bullshit.

I tell you now, "I'm goin out an rob a bank," right? "Go down on Park Avenue an stick that bank up." I go down there, I don stick that bank up. Somethin stop me.

Then I say, "Tomorrow, I'm goin down there, stick that bank up. Stead of goin down eleven o'clock, I'm goin down there four o'clock." I go down there four o'clock, an the bank's closed. There it is again. Damn.

"I'm goin down there the day after tomorrow. I'm gonna rob that bank." You go down there day after tomorrow, git hit by a car, wind up in the hospital. Thas the future for you. Thas the way I look at it.

You can plan all kinds of things. You can plan anything in the world. An nine out of ten, you make plans, ain't nothin gonna come through. My grandmother tole me when I was a boy, like as knocked ma shoes off, she said, "You can plan an plan an wish and wish, but shit in one hand an plan an wish in the other an see what you feel first." Thas it right there. Thas the whole thing.

Marble, Colorado

I t is a very mountainous, very remote territory. The road, mostly gravel, winds over small wooden bridges and mountain creeks, past an occasional gas station and general store. It is a refreshing change from all the imitation Swiss mountaineer shops lining the streets of Aspen, where the road begins.

Charlie Orlosky and his wife Marjorie chose to spend their lives in the remote shadows of the mountain, where the winters are mild, because they love and know the wilderness. When I meet them, they are both in their late sixties, and both are trappers.* They have lived all their life surrounded by snow-covered mountains, clear streams, and wild animals, and have managed to become so knowledgeable that they are able to survive completely off what they find there; and most of the time they do.

They are very reluctant about any publicity, and it took some persuasion on the telephone for them to let me come out and talk to them. When I arrive, they greet me graciously. Mrs. Orlosky is petite and pretty; her eyes sparkle with a special life when she talks about their life together. One gets an extraordinary sense of the togetherness of this kind of remote living, which is underlined when Mr. Orlosky, with a soft smile, talks about how in his early years he had one partner, and then he looks at her and says, "but then I got a permanent partner." They are full of enthusiasm as they talk about going out in the winter laying trap lines, an arduous process, which means sometimes being alone for days, snow-shoeing through the mountains to meet in the shacks they have erected along the trap lines. There they prepare the animal skins and rest before moving on. They have a kind of peace about themselves that may partly explain the fact that they never feel lonely. They are constantly involved in doing or making something. And they seem to love all the things as well as the animals that surround them. Mr. Orlosky made most of the furniture in the house; and Mrs. Orlosky bakes, cooks, pickles, and preserves most of their food. When she invites me to stay for some biscuits she is baking—"they're real good"—I *know* they are something very special and regret I have to think about something as dull as a long drive to an airport.

They are full of knowledge about living out-of-doors, and Mr. Orlosky has been asked many times to speak at the Colorado Outdoor Survival School. He is a soft-spoken, wiry man with thickly muscled forearms. He talks about trapping with excitement and concern, and about the threat of the federally sponsored poison programs with fury. Much of the poisoning is indiscriminately killing off valuable wild-

---

Editor's note: A few months later, Mr. Orlosky died of a heart attack.

life, such as the eagle, and destroying important ecological balances. The ignorance embodied in the program enrages him as much as its cruelty. He has spent much of his life trying to educate people.

Both the Orloskys reveal the kind of wisdom so many people today are actively seeking in the return-to-the-land movement. They learned a lot of what they know firsthand, through years of experiment and careful observation; the rest, secondhand, from Mr. Orlosky's parents. There is centuries-old knowledge here, the kind of things perhaps only a handful of people in the entire country know.

Charles and Marjorie Orlosky

CHARLIE: My folks moved here in nineteen-oh-nine. I was four years old at the time. My dad worked in the mill. First he was a marble crater, where they crated the marble after it was finished. And then he became a diamond-saw expert—he sawed marble with a diamond saw. And when I worked in the mill, I was a crane operator and worked there most of the year. My job at the mill was operating an overhead traveling crane—that's where we lifted the blocks around, turned them over and load the gang saws. I have worked in the quarries, but at the quarry I worked as a jack-hammer man up there.

In Marble is where the marble works were. We had the largest finishing plant in the world at that time. We lived over in town then. And we built this place after the works shut down. Marble shut down in about nineteen forty-one. We didn't buy this place until about ten years later.

We'd lived off the land before that. See, like during the depression days, I worked nine days in three years for wages. So we had to live off the land then of course. So for an instance, we'd get wood out of the river, driftwood for firewood in the wintertime. The stove was a fifty-five-gallon oil drum. And it worked very well, because we could put a big root in there, see, a big stump of some kind, and we could regulate it, and we could open up a draft in the morning, and it would take right off.

MARGE: We'd leave ashes in the bottom of our stove, just in the bottom of the barrel—actually it was layin on its side. And then you just built a fire in it with kindlin and paper and git it to goin, and then you can put a stump in there, and you can keep it goin all winter and not start another fire.

CHARLIE: Long time ago, I taught myself how to trap by trial and error. Learned to do it myself and from what I could read on it. Well, first I started out with muskrats when I was eight years old. And then I had one trap. I still have it. And I've caught as high as four muskrats one day in that one trap by lookin at it early in the mornin, at noon, an then after school, an then late in the evening. Well, it's just a number one Victor trap. It's a long spring. Of course, them days, traps were built a lot better than they are now. A trap nowadays wouldn't last near that long. So then started trappin mink and weasel.

We don't have any mink now, but we used to have quite a number of em. They all disappeared. Haven't seen a mink track now fer, oh, I guess, five years.

You make your sets to suit each animal, you know. And fer bait, well, later as we got better at it, we used scent practically altogether. Each animal has a different type of scent that you use for em. Of course, when I was a kid, I used bait— meat, fish or sumpin to ketch mink with, an carrots an apples an stuff to ketch muskrats with. But muskrats, we would try to set it on their slides—where they have slides—and ketch them that way. The main idea with muskrat trapping is to set your traps where they will drown. Otherwise, they twist their front foot off in just a matter of hours and get away. They survive most of the time. And it depends on how bad they break up their teeth in the trap. If they break em up real bad, why then they'll starve, because they don't have their front teeth to work with. So we don't like to leg any animal. Try to fix the trap so they'll drown or ketch em by hind leg. But now we have more modern traps that kill em instantly. They are known as the conibear trap, and they work very well for muskrats an beaver both.

Now a beaver has a special scent that's right in him, you know. We use that for other beaver. These are glands, that we take out of the animal to use to ketch other animals. There are separate scent glands in a beaver, so that's what we use. And it's the stuff the beaver used to stake out their boundaries. And any other beaver that smells it will come an investigate it to see what that smell means. It's just like you notice how dogs will do. They have to leave a scent. They don't read newspapers, so they have to leave a scent some other way.

Then from muskrats on to mink an then beaver. Of course in them days we weren't allowed to ketch beaver. But there has always been beaver poaching going on, you know, for years, until, oh, the last fifteen, twenty years there wasn't much, because it's legal now to trap beaver. We work on a permit system or make a deal with private landowners.

We have some land and we trap for other landowners as well. And then we get permits from the Game and Fish Department to trap on public land. We trap mainly beaver now and a few bobcats, or lynx cats, as we call em. But other furs aren't worth bothering with. Some muskrats. But you take a marten, it used to bring us a twenty-dollar average or twenty-five-dollar average, now will average you about five dollars.

In the marten case, they can't compete with the Russian sable—Russian sable is a specie of the same animal, but the fur is so much denser and heavier and darker that our marten can't compete with it. And it's been coming into this country, as I understand it, duty free. So nobody'll buy our marten, since they can buy a Russian sable. There seem to be some attraction of foreign furs, too. They seem to rather buy it when it comes from a foreign country than if it originates in this country.

So that's the reason that our marten is down. And then of course for years a coyote wasn't worth anything—any long-hair fur. It went out of style. But it seems like it's making a revival now. So some of your long fur are coming back.

After you'd learned to trap animals, you can trap about any animal there is. Of course, we'll start with the muskrat, then the mink and the weasel and the marten, then the fox and the coyote. We didn't have many badger. We trapped a few of them. Don't trap any kind for their meat. And then, of course, I've trapped a lot of bear when I worked for the government, and killed a few on my own. I guess that's about the size of the animals that we have around here.

MARGE: We used to save all the bear fat, though, and use it for frying doughnuts, making cookies, and all that kind of stuff. You can't beat it.

CHARLIE: We used to eat bear meat, too, until I found out what they actually live on a lot.

We killed a female one year that had—well, we got seventy pounds of rendered-out lard out of her, and her meat was real good. So about two weeks later I killed a big male, a real big one. So I brought it home and skinned it. It was in the fall of the year, so the meat kind of froze a little bit and would keep good.

So people would come down and want some bear meat. So Marge cut em off a chunk of this—the males are called boars and the females are called sows—so she would cut a chunk of this boar off and give it to the people. So one day she thought she would try it, too, and she fried some steaks off the old male for us to eat. And then the first bite I knew there was something wrong with it.

MARGE: Well, I knew it almost when I was cooking it. It was so strong.

CHARLIE: And it burned my throat when I swallowed it, it was so strong. Fortunately, we had a police dog that loved bear meat, which is kind of unusual in itself, I think. So it got most of that bear. But then after that we just didn't kind of like bear any more. And then when I found out that they'll just, oh, eat maggots by the bushel, any rotten meat that they can find. They're more or less a carrion-eater in the summertime. In the wintertime they hibernate. In the fall they eat berries and shrubs and things like that, you know. They'll eat anything. See, their molars are built more like a human molar than a canine. They have flat teeth for molars. They have their tusks, but, so, they can eat anything. They can be vegetarian or they can be meat-eaters. And so in the fall when there's a lot of berries and stuff, they fatten up on them berries and acorns and stuff. Lots of berries.

MARGE: Like your mountain ash. He just stands up on his hind legs—and they're in big clusters—he just gets up there at a branch and puts it in one side of his mouth and pulls it out the other, and all the berries are in his mouth, see.

CHARLIE: Then he blows the leaves out, like that, chews up the berries. We've watched em eat up close. They're quite an animal. And of course the hide's never worth much. All that it's used for is, oh, you know, like rugs or stuff like that. But then the lard, we used to use it a lot. We always had bear lard around for cooking purposes, and it's kind of a soft grease.

MARGE: Yeah, unless you get it cold, it never gets real hard. It's kind of a runny-type lard.

CHARLIE: Of course, you gut it first and clean it out good. Then you have to skin it and cut the fat off. The fat's between the hide and the carcass. And I've heard of bears having ten inches of fat on their back, but I've never seen any quite that fat. The fattest one we ever got had four inches of fat surrounding the body, mainly on the back and belly. That's quite a bit of lard itself. Then we cut it into cubes and render it out.

MARGE: I always use just a great big dishpan. You put a little lard in first or you can put a little water in it to begin with, in your fat. And then you just add a fire under it and just keep working at it until it all renders out.

CHARLIE: What's left is a grease, just like oil, that's what it is. And then the cracklings, of course—that's the stuff that don't render out. You throw them away, strain out this lard, and then when it hardens, it turns white. That's the way they make pork lard, too, the same way. And then we used to mix a little bit of deer tallow in it, once in a while, to make it more solid. On a bear it's fat, and on a deer it's tallow. Deer and sheep it's tallow. But some of these big bucks used to get three inches of tallow on their backs, too, in the fall. So we used to make use of all that stuff. I wouldn't kill a bear now even if we had one right here in my yard, which we do have occasionally.

I've killed so many of them, I wouldn't wanna—and they're getting scarce. The sheep men are killing em off just as fast as they can. And so I haven't killed a bear for some years and have no intention of killing another one.

One thing that would help us an awful lot would be if they would get rid of all the poison that they use to control animals with, because poison in any form is not selective, and it kills animals that it is not intended to kill. So until we get rid of all the poison, why—

The Bureau of Fisheries and Wildlife and a lot of private individuals put it out, especially this Thalium that has killed so many eagles in Wyoming. Thalium poison is a very cruel, extremely cruel and slow poison, and the government quit using it years ago because it was so dangerous and so cruel. But the sheep men were allowed to buy all they want of it up until now, and they have been putting it out all the time. They are trying to kill off all the coyotes.

MARGE: They are trying to kill off most anything that bothers the sheep.

CHARLIE: They don't want nothing left alive except their sheep, and that's the way it would seem, you know. They just want everything killed off. A lot of their problem today is that they can't get herders. You see, the old herders are too old to hire and the new ones don't want to take a job at herdin sheep. And why should they when they can go out here and work for great big wages? And they don't want to be stuck up there in the mountains with all that loneliness and everything for small wages, which I think they only get two hundred and fifty or three hundred dollars a month now at the most. So they just don't have the herders. So several of these sheep men that have more than one band of sheep are just turnin em loose, nobody to protect the herds. And somebody comes and salts em every once in a while. So if there's any predators around, why they can have a free hand to work at em. And whatever causes that sheep's death—it doesn't have to be a coyote or a bear—the coyote or bear gets blamed for it.

The government says, "Oh we put these poison stations up where it doesn't bother the fur-bearing animals, the smaller ones," but that's not true, because they have no way to control that poison. You take for instance a coyote that feeds on a ten-eighty station, when he gets sick, he'll start running—not like a dog: a dog will scream and holler—and a coyote will go for miles and he will vomit several times. They will try to get rid of everything that's in their stomach. And every place that he vomits is another poison station. And whatever finds that vomit will eat it. I don't know why an animal will eat a vomit quicker than he will something else. So there's no way to control it. See, this coyote may be several miles from where he picked it up. He may be in timber and along river banks or somewhere and vomit along in there. So anything that finds that, like a marten or a weasel or mink, is going to eat it, and then he'll die. So there's no way to control it whatsoever.

And then when they kill off all the coyotes or most of em, the rodents take over. And there will be areas where they'll be places in the high country that look like that just got through plowin on it. Even a horse will sink clear up to his belly in some of that, where the gophers and field mice have ruined the country, dug it all up. So then they have to come in there with this ten-eighty poison grain to kill off the rodents. Then that finishes off all the animals, such as weasel and marten and skunks and stuff like that, badger.

Years ago when we had worlds of coyotes and a lot more sheep than we got now, they didn't have this predator problem that they have nowdays. But by putting poison in everything that died, you know—they'd have a dead sheep, deer or whatever they had, they'd put poison in it. They would put poison out all winter long in sheep carcasses and horse carcasses. The coyote had to learn to survive. He had to kill his food and not eat anything that was dead. Yeah, the sheep man has hurt himself in that respect.

So now that they've created the problem, I don't think that all the other animals should be killed off just to satisfy a few sheep men.

MARGE: We haven't had a redtail hawk here all summer long. They kill off your rodents, see. And for years we've had an eagle and his mate around here, and he was huge—he was an awful big fellow. And we'd feed him in the wintertime, carcasses, you know, that we'd trapped. About three years ago he and his mate disappeared. They were poisoned, we found out. There was poison put up here that year.

It's just awful the way they've just kept a-goin and a-goin, and the first thing you know we'll have nothin but frogs.

CHARLIE: I'm retired now as far as workin's concerned. Otherwise, I draw my social security, which isn't very much. So I guess you'd call me retired. We still work and carry on, trap a little bit. I want to keep active as long as I possibly can, so I do what I can.

When I lived in town I would have to start real early in the morning. And I had a good trap-line horse. We called him Jim. That's one that was trained for the

trap line, you know. And I'd have to leave early in the morning, because it'd be a long, cold day, and I wouldn't get back till after dark.

You have to take all your bait and your scent along with you and some traps. A lot of your traps would be covered up with snow. You'd have to dig em all out and reset em for the next trip. Most of the animals are dead. The small animals just die overnight, just freeze. They don't live hardly any length of time. Like a marten and weasel, you hardly ever find one of them alive in a trap. They fight so hard that they just die in a little while. But I never shoot an animal in a trap. If he's still alive, I just knock him in the head. I generally have a hatchet or something or a diggin tool that I use to set my traps with. Just hit em and stun em and then I'd stomp on their heart with my heel. That'd be the coyotes and the fox. And they die very shortly. And it don't seem to be too painful either. It just break their hearts. So then anything that we could that way, why, we'd skin it while it was warm. But then, well, with snow we'd have to break the trail out for the horse, let him pick his own way. We had a real good horse for that. And take care of all the traps. It's cold work, awful cold work. And you'd get on and off so many times a day, you know.

We would be out maybe for three or four months at a time in the winter. Livin out in the hill. We'd generally be on snowshoes from daylight till about dark every day. She'd run her own trap lines, and I'd run my own. But we'd try to be in the next camp so we'd be together at night. We'd try to make a circle affair, you know. We had three camps: like we had one tent possibly and then we'd use prospectors' cabins for the other camp. We'd fix them up. And then we'd have supplies in each camp. And then we'd have roundabout ways to git there. And we'd try to make a big circle so we wouldn't have to keep followin the same line all the time. And we wouldn't see anybody at all for three months.

MARGE: Bein apart all day long does a lot to break up the monotony of bein with each other, you know.

CHARLIE: And then you try to go out every day, even if it's stormin real bad. You got to take care of your furs. So on storming days we could do some of that. You see, when they're skinned, then they have to be fleshed, and then they're stretched and dried. So that takes quite a little time itself, where you have quite a lot of fur to take care of. So we'd try to set one day aside in one of our better camps to take care of furs.

MARGE: We had one camp, we had a pretty good stove in there, a pretty nice cabin. I'd wash, and he'd generally stretch the furs. And we'd do anything that needed to be done, you know. We couldn't be movin around, like in a tent, you can't do that.

CHARLIE: After we come back down, why we'd ship the furs. We used to wait till about January. You can only really trap in the winter when the furs are in their prime, like say from November until the last of January is about the best time. Then your beaver and your muskrat are best in the spring of the year when your ice melts off. And your bobcats are better, best, in February and March. They don't prime up as fast as the rest of em do. Then fox, you don't want to trap them very late in the winter, because they start rubbing—their hips get rubbed, see, where they sit down in the snow. And every time they sit down a hair or two freezes to the snow, and they pull it out. And then finally they get two little spots there where the guard hair is gone on their rump. And that's what they call a rubbed fox. And if they are rubbed quite badly, they knock off the price. So we try never to trap them too late in the season. And November and December is the best time for fox.

In the summer, of course, we were gettin ready for the winter, like putting in our wood supply, our hay supply. And we'd do a lot of scoutin around the mountains to locate furs, you know, to see where we was goin to trap in the following fall. And then there had to be the scent made, which was quite a little problem in itself. You have to rot the stuff, the flesh baits and all. And well then, of course, we'd have to fish some. We ate fish, too. We'd raise a pig or two.

MARGE: And raise an occasional bum lamb. They'd have to be taken care of. And then in the fall we'd butcher the pigs and cure them, smoke the hams and bacon and make sausage with some pork and deer or elk or whatever we had, and hang them up and smoke them and put the garden stuff away. A pig. Well, we didn't waste anything on a pig but the hair and the squeal, as they say.

We eat the skin, you know. You scald a pig and take the hair off, and then you can eat the skin. It's real good with different types of vegetables. You boil it. Like we make sour turnips. Well, sour turnips is made just like sour kraut, only it's cut in thinner strips. It's wonderful with sour turnips. You just cut it in strips, take off the fat to make the lard, and then you take and cut the skin in strips, and whenever you want sour turnips or something, you just cook it like you would boil cabbage or anything with it.

We make blood sausage. We make our own casing out of the pig, out of his intestines—clean them, wash them and everything. Then we make our blood sausage with rice and peppermint leaves, you know. Just put a little bit in with the rice and the blood, the solid part of the blood. And then put it in the casings and then boil it, and then when we were ready to use it, why then we'd put it in the oven with a little bit of grease and kind of fry it, brown it a little bit. Delicious. His mother taught me a lot of this.

CHARLIE: My mother lived off the land a lot. Of course, she came from Europe, where they didn't have much out there, you know. So she had to learn to make use of every little thing there was. They were from Yugoslavia, and my dad and her both came from over there. So they had tough pickins. Wages was real cheap in the olden days, and so they had to make everything count. She couldn't waste a thing.

We live on wild meat even today. We don't buy . . .

MARGE: The only thing we buy is chicken. We never buy meat.

CHARLIE: I kill an elk every fall and a deer, and that will keep us in meat until the next hunting season. Of course an elk is a pretty large animal. And then Marge raises all of her garden stuff, and she done that for years.

MARGE: Potatoes and cabbages—make sour kraut—and turnips.

CHARLIE: She raises a lot of stuff to give away.

MARGE: Freeze. Now we freeze instead of canning. We freeze green beans and put my carrots in a big crock we have. They keep all winter long.

CHARLIE: Big pottery crock, made of pottery.

MARGE: I just wad up a few newspapers in the bottom and wash them and put my carrots in there and then put a little plastic over the top, and they keep all winter just as crisp and nice as can be in the cellar. We have two cellars, one outside and one under the house. You have to have cellars up here to keep your vegetables and things from freezing.

I think it would be wonderful, young kids doing this today, if they would leave alone what belonged to you. But so many of them thinks what belongs to you is theirs, too. That makes it bad. I heard the other day that the hippy generation now are going around and they pick people's asparagus that grows wild on their ditch banks, you know, or any berries or anything. They're just stripping stuff.

CHARLIE: One objection is they fill the ditches up with dirt. People wouldn't mind them cuttin their asparagus, I'm sure, but they throw the debris into the ditches, see, clogs up the ditches.

MARGE: They need some training, and they should be trained. If they would listen and be trained and take care of themselves like they should, I think it would be wonderful. And a lot of them are. They really are. They're trying very hard to live like they used to, which I think, is a very good idea.

I used to pick lots of berries before there got too many people in the hills. Now you can't go out but what you don't run into a bunch of people. And I don't like it. So I hardly ever really get out and pick berries. I just pick em around here or maybe I'll go down with somebody else from the ranch and pick some berries. Like people down here, they went down and got me some choke cherries yesterday. So I'll cook my choke cherries and strain my juice out and can it. And this winter when I need choke-cherry juice, why I'll make jelly with it.

You just cook the berries. You put water in them and cook em and then you strain it out through a cloth. That's the way to get juice out. And then you just throw the berry part away, cause choke cherries has pretty good seed in them. And then I just can them up in quart jars, hot, with no sugar or anything in it, just can it up. And then when I need jelly, why then I just make up some jelly. We have Oregon grape and choke cherries and raspberries and thimble berries—it's a good deal like a raspberry only richer. And I guess we even have a few wild blueberries up here in this country.

Now I don't know a whole lot about herbs. If I get herbs, I generally send for them. Used to be we'd use, oh, mustard plaster, which all older people did, you know, if you had a cold or you had pneumonia. Or if Charlie's been out in the hills—well, his brother was with him one time, and he caught a bad cold. So Charlie made onion syrup. You'd sweeten it and boil the onion—cut it up and put some water with it and boil it. And onion syrup was quite the thing in those days for clearing a cold. But Charlie didn't have but the one onion. So he made him up some stuff out of pine boughs, and boiled it, you know, and he drank that. Well, he got over his cold the next morning, I guess. It was pretty bitter, but he got over it. Just take some pine needles and boil them. Of course, that would be quite strong.

And then we have the balsam pine up here, smooth trunk, and they have blisters on them. And we'd go gather the blisters for winter with little jars in the fall. It's a pitch, you know, kind of runny, clear pitch. Just put it on a cut or anything and put a piece of cloth over it and trim it off around the edge of the cloth, and we'd leave that to heal.

You learn from reading and you learn from experience. Like his mother—one of our horses one time had run a roofing nail up his hoof. It was pretty bad. So she showed up with little round leaves. I know tansy is good, but I still don't know this little leaf that she had him, after he got the nail out, put up in the hoof, you know, to heal the thing. I know what it is, but I don't know the name of it.

People learn from experience and from each other. I think in the olden times, people would hand it down just like your Indians. They'd hand down their

180.

legends and things. And the older people handed down their recipes for, say, making soap.

Now that's another thing I used to do: I used to make all my own soap. I don't anymore. I prefer detergents. I just like the way detergents work better than I do soap. Then we have a small, hand, flour mill, and we'd grind our corn up for cornmeal and wheat. But we'd have to buy the corn and the wheat both. Can't grow it here. And we'd grind up flour. We didn't use so much. I didn't use it for breads, but I'd use it for pancakes and things like that. Make wonderful pancakes. And I still use sour dough for pancakes in the mornings.

Well, you just sour your dough. You start it off with a little yeast and flour and water, and you set it up close to the stove with the lid off, cause they say there's so much wild yeast in the air. Then you just set it up there and you leave it sit for thirty-six hours or so. And it gets a tang to it. And then when you get ready to make your pancakes, you pour a little bit of this in a bowl, the way I do it. Now most of the people don't do it this way. I keep quite a little sour dough on hand. Most of the people, just a cupful.

Well then you add a little bit, just a little bit, of sugar and salt, and then after you put that in, then you put, oh, for just the two of us, I put in maybe not quite a quarter of a teaspoonful of baking soda. And that kind of boils up. And when that gets through boiling, then I put in, oh, a couple tablespoonfuls of salad oil and some dry milk. We don't care for egg in pancake. I learnt that during the depression. We didn't have the eggs. So. And then just fry them. They make wonderful pancakes.

I've had my present sour dough now, oh, I imagine, a good two years, maybe three. It'll keep. You can put it in the refrigerator when you don't use it. But if we're working or anything we always have pancakes for breakfast, cause toast don't stay with you very long. We're not much for eating breakfast foods or anything like that.

As a rule, most everything I have on my table, like peas, are grown here. I had some kids in that were on their honeymoon up here one time, and they stayed in our little cabin, and I hadn't thought about it, but I made biscuits—my biscuits are supposed to be real good. And I had biscuits, and I had dried corn, I think, that I had dried, you know. We had wild meat and my own potatoes and salad.

You know, you dry your corn, and then you cook it. The real way to do dried corn is to husk it and everything and put it in a big boiler, like you used to boil your clothes in when you washed. And you'd just put your corn in there and bring it to a boil till you set the milk in the kernels. And then you cut that all off, scrape the cob, and then you put it up on a roof or someplace hot on cheesecloth, on a frame, where the air will get to it and let it set till it dries. And then you put it away in jars. And then when you are ready to use it, why you just put it on. Before, you soak it overnight. You just boil it with a little water, and it takes quite a while to cook the real dry corn, and a little butter with it and salt and pepper. It's simply delicious. It's got a wonderful flavor to it. I made some last fall, but now I boil it—take it right off the cob and I cook it with a little sugar and milk and till it's dry in the pan. And then I put it on cookie sheets and put it in the oven and finish dryin it that way. That way it only takes about half an hour to cook it.

Afterword

This book is not a comprehensive sociological study of subsistence living in the United States. Rather, it suggests the resourcefulness of a handful of individuals, scattered across the country, east and west, north and south.

A Ford Foundation travel and research grant made it possible to send Carol DeChellis Hill and Bruce Davidson around the country in pursuit of people of character and determination, people whose stubbornness marks them as pioneers.

With the help of researcher Patty Neuwirth, we followed up leads provided by federal agencies, community-action groups, newspaper articles, and friends. Ken Rosen, a poet and teacher who lives in Maine, led us to Russell Hayes. Patty traced down an Office of Economic Opportunity local contact list to find Eugenia Thompson. Friends in Colorado Springs referred us to the Orloskys, who were known in the area for their skills in hunting and trapping. Newspaper articles led us to Charlie Fitzgerald and Bigtown.

Some of our leads fell through. The madame of a whore house in Peoria, Illinois and the leader of the local motorcycle gang were driven underground by police a day or two before Carol was scheduled to arrive. A black man whose parents had been slaves in North Carolina, was hard of hearing but could make out the words of a friend whose speech was especially familiar. She acted as his "translator," when he told Carol how he had gone to see evangelist Billy Graham but could not hear him until he began to speak the truth. Finally, the use of an intermediary proved too awkward for our purposes.

Some of the people in the book lead very private lives and have come to value that privacy. Out of respect for their feelings, we changed their names and the names of the towns in which they live.

There were of course frustrating moments when our method proved inadequate and we somehow failed to touch or record the people we encountered. Bunt Howard of Greasy Creek, Kentucky was one of these. His Appalachian mountain reticence made conversation an absurdity. Instead, his son played clamorous dulcimer music into the tape recorder. Yet the Howards belong in this book, because they persist in isolation, in a stubborn determination to live as they know best, making baskets, chairs, houses, music, working proudly to do what must be done.

Our difficulty in communicating with them taught us how isolated people can be in twentieth-century America. It made us wonder, too, about the facility with which sociologists sometimes write about "the underprivileged," quoting them at length, these people for whom words are flimsier than baskets, not much good for holding things of value.

We learned that there are different languages in this country—not just dialects, but languages. A lesson taught us by the Howards and driven home by the peculiar code of the hobos. Bigtown showed Carol a few hobo signs, which we confirmed in Henry Dreyfuss's Book of Symbols, and reproduce here.

There are recipes, too, little formulae for dealing with the world. Baskets, dulcimer music, sausages, medicine, red ochre, biscuits, road signs, windmills, baked beans, welding irons, a grinding wheel—these are the elements of a subsistence language that we can only begin to decipher.

—*Jamie Shalleck*